Colorado Wildlife

Written and Illustrated
by Todd Telander

FALCONGUIDES ®

GUILFORD, CONNECTICUT
HELENA, MONTANA

AN IMPRINT OF GLOBE PEQUOT PRESS

To my wife, Kirsten, my children, Miles and Oliver, and my parents,
all of whom have supported and encouraged me through the years.

FALCONGUIDES®

Copyright © 2014 Morris Book Publishing, LLC
Illustrations copyright © 2014 Todd Telander

FalconGuides is an imprint of Globe Pequot Press.
Falcon, FalconGuides, and Outfit Your Mind are registered trademarks of Morris
Book Publishing, LLC.

Illustrations: Todd Telander
Project Editor: Staci Zacharski
Text Design: Sheryl P. Kober
Layout Artist: Sue Murray

Library of Congress Cataloging-in-Publication Data is available on file.

ISBN 978-0-7627-8496-7

Printed in the United States of America

10 9 8 7 6 5 4 3 2 1

Contents

Introduction

Colorado is a region of vast diversity, and home to some of North America's most fascinating wildlife. The great Rocky Mountains flank the Continental Divide, which runs down the state's center and separates the vast Great Plains on the east from the high, arid plateaus to the west. This geographic diversity provides for an incredible variety and number of animal species, and gives wildlife enthusiasts a unique opportunity to see animals of both western and eastern North America, whose ranges intersect here. In its high altitude tundra, montane parks, grasslands, river canyons, and desert sage lands, Colorado provides a home to thousands of species. This guide describes some of the more common and interesting mammals, birds, fish, reptiles, amphibians, and butterflies you are likely to encounter in the state, and includes some found only in this area.

Notes about the Species Accounts

Names

Both the common name and the scientific name are included for
each entry. Since common names tend to vary regionally, and
there may be more than one common name for each species, the
universally accepted scientific name of genus and species (such
as *Nucifraga columbiana* for the Clark's nutcracker) is a reliable
way to be certain of identification. Also, you can learn interesting
facts about an animal by understanding the English translation of
its Latin name. For instance, the generic name, *nucifraga,* derives
from the Latin *nucis,* meaning nut, and *fraga,* meaning to break.

Size

Most measurements of size refer to overall length, from nose
to tail tip. For animals with very long tails, antennae, or other
appendages, measurements for those parts may be given sepa-
rately from those of the body. Butterfly and moth measurements
refer to wingspan. Size may vary considerably within a species
(due to age, sex, or environmental conditions), so use this mea-
surement as a general guide, not a rule.

Range

Range refers to the geographical area where a species is likely to
be found, such as western Colorado, in the Rocky Mountains, in
eastern Colorado, etc. Some species may be found throughout
their range, whereas others prefer very specific habitats within
the range. The season during which the species is present in Colorado is also mentioned under this heading. For migratory birds,
and for some butterflies, the season is the time when the great-
est number of individuals can be found in the area. Some species are year-round residents, some may spend only summers or
winters in the state, and some may be transient, only stopping
during spring or fall migrations. Even if only part of the year is
indicated for a species, be aware that there may be individuals

that arrive earlier or remain longer than the given time frame. Most land-dwelling animals are year-round residents. Some fish may arrive in seasonal migrations.

Habitat

An animal's habitat is one of the first clues to its identification. Note the environment (including vegetation, climate, elevation, substrate, presence or absence of water) and compare it with the description listed for the animal. Some common habitats in Colorado include prairies, pine forests, alpine meadows, tundra, foothills, sage lands, chaparral, rivers and streams, urban areas, and grasslands.

Illustrations

The illustrations show adult animals in the colorations they are most likely to have in Colorado. Many species show variation in different geographical areas, in different seasons, or between the sexes. Birds show this variety most often, so I have illustrated males and females when they look different. Other variations, such as seasonal color changes in some mammals and variable patterns in fish, are described in the text.

Useful Scientific Terms

I have, for the most part, used familiar language to describe the animals in this book, but there are occasions when it makes more sense to use terms developed by the scientific community, especially when referring to body parts. In particular, terms and characteristics associated with birds, reptiles, amphibians, fish, and butterflies are described below:

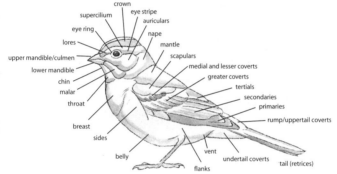

Lizards

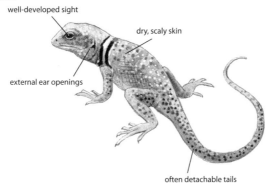

well-developed sight

dry, scaly skin

external ear openings

often detachable tails

Snakes

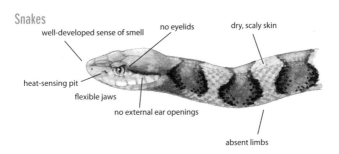

well-developed sense of smell

no eyelids

dry, scaly skin

heat-sensing pit

flexible jaws

no external ear openings

absent limbs

Turtles

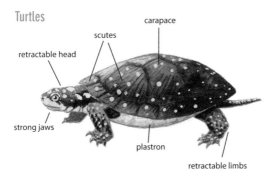

carapace

scutes

retractable head

strong jaws

plastron

retractable limbs

Frogs

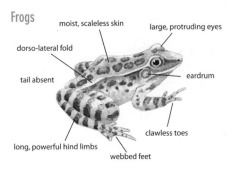

moist, scaleless skin

large, protruding eyes

dorso-lateral fold

tail absent

eardrum

clawless toes

long, powerful hind limbs

webbed feet

Toads

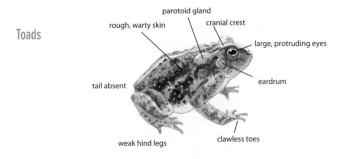

parotoid gland

rough, warty skin

cranial crest

large, protruding eyes

tail absent

eardrum

weak hind legs

clawless toes

Salamanders

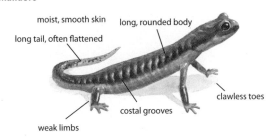

moist, smooth skin

long, rounded body

long tail, often flattened

clawless toes

weak limbs

costal grooves

Fish

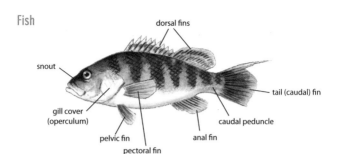

dorsal fins

snout

gill cover (operculum)

pelvic fin

pectoral fin

anal fin

caudal peduncle

tail (caudal) fin

Butterflies

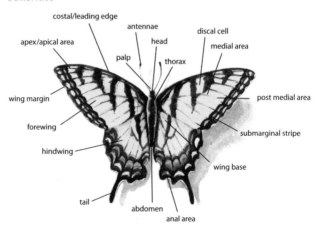

costal/leading edge

antennae

discal cell

apex/apical area

palp

head

medial area

thorax

wing margin

post medial area

forewing

submarginal stripe

hindwing

wing base

tail

abdomen

anal area

MAMMALS

Virginia Opossum, *Didelphis virginiana*
Family Didelphidae (Opossums)
Size: 30" with tail
Range: Throughout eastern Colorado
Habitat: Woodlands, riparian zones, urban areas with trees, farms

The Virginia opossum is a marsupial, meaning it bears premature young that develop in an external pouch, and is the only member of this group in North America. It is stocky, with relatively small limbs, a pointed snout, and a long, round, hairless tail. Its color is mottled grayish, with a white face and dark ears. It is nocturnal, mostly solitary, and reasonably adept at swimming and climbing. It has a highly varied diet that includes nuts, fruit, insects, small animals, and carrion. Opossums have a curious habit of feigning death when under attack, then resuming as normal once safe.

Southern Short-tailed Shrew, *Blarina carolinensis*
Family Soricidae (Shrews)
Size: 3-5" long with tail
Range: Northeastern Colorado
Habitat: Moist woodlands, brushy areas

Shrews are the smallest mammals in North America, and are unrelated to the rodents. The southern short-tailed shrew is very active. It is shaped like a long mouse, with a sharply pointed head, tiny eyes, no external ears, and a short, lightly furred tail. Its fur is dense, dark gray above and slightly paler below. This shrew is active day and night, mostly solitary, and utilizes an extensive network of tunnels, which it digs itself. Voracious feeders, shrews forage within their tunnels and nearby leaf litter for insects, earthworms, spiders, small invertebrates, and sometimes nuts and seeds. Shrews can also secrete a poisonous saliva that paralyzes prey.

Eastern Mole, *Scalopus aquaticus*
Family Talpidae (True Moles)
Size: 6" long with tail
Range: Far eastern Colorado
Habitat: A variety, including fields, woodlands, lawns, and areas with dry, loose soils

Also known as the common mole, the eastern mole is a small, stocky, sturdy mammal with a body well designed for life underground. It is elongate and tube-shaped, with narrow hips, a pointed, fleshy snout, and a short tail. Its fur is short, velvety, deep gray-brown above and slightly paler below. Its eyes are tiny and covered by skin, and its ears are invisible beneath its fur. Eastern moles build tunnels, which they dig with their broad, spadelike forelimbs and long, thick claws. They forage within the tunnels for earthworms, insects, and some plants. Eastern moles are responsible for creating conspicuous dirt mounds at the entrances to their tunnels.

Big Brown Bat, *Eptesicus fuscus*
Family Vespertilionidae (Vespertilionid Bats)
Size: 5" with tail
Range: Throughout Colorado
Habitat: A wide variety, including woodlands, buildings, and caves

As a group, bats are the only mammals that truly fly, using wings made of a thin membrane stretched across elongated forearms and fingers. The big brown bat is widely distributed. It is fairly large, with fur that is brown above and lighter below, with blackish wing membranes. There is a fleshy projection at the base of the ear (the tragus), which is short and rounded. Big brown bats are nocturnal, roosting by day in dark, secluded areas such as caves or old buildings. They emerge at night to forage for beetles and other insects, locating them primarily by echolocation, emitting high-pitched chirps and receiving reflected sound with their complex, large ears.

Brazilian Free-tailed Bat, *Tadarida brasiliensis*
Family Molossidae (Free-tailed Bats)
Size: ~4" with tail
Range: Throughout Colorado
Habitat: Caves, buildings, and surrounding environs

Also known as the Mexican free-tailed bat or guano bat, the Brazilian free-tailed bat is small, with narrow wings and a tail that projects freely about halfway past the interfemoral membrane, a patch of skin that stretches between the legs. Its fur is rich brown, slightly darker above than below, and its wings are blackish. The ears are broad, reaching forward on the face, and the upper snout is wrinkled. Brazilian free-tailed bats emerge from roosting sites at night in large groups, and forage in the air for a variety of insects, using echolocation to zero in on prey. These bats are among the most numerous mammals in the United States, famous for gathering in enormous concentrations in caves in New Mexico, and for depositing deep accumulations of guano in those caves.

American Pika, *Ochotona princeps*
Family Ochotonidae (Pikas)
Size: ~8" long
Range: Mountainous Colorado
Habitat: Rocky slopes at high altitudes

The pika is a small, plump resident of the mountains, and is related to the rabbits. It has a relatively large head, rounded ears, and a tiny tail that is usually not visible in the field. Its fur is thick and pale grayish brown. It is often detected by its high-pitched, squeaking call. The pika makes tunnels through the snow in winter that leave traces on the ground upon snowmelt. Active during the day, mostly solitary and moving about in slow bounds, pikas forage on grasses and herbs, which they store in large piles, like hay, for the lean winter months.

Snowshoe Hare, *Lepus americanus*
Family Leporidae (Rabbits and Hares)
Size/Weight: ~15" long/~3 lbs
Range: Mountainous Colorado
Habitat: Forests, mountains, swamps

The snowshoe hare is found in the mountains. It has long ears, a short, round tail, and especially large rear feet that give traction in snow. During the summer it is grayish brown with a pale underside, while in the winter its fur becomes snow white, except for large, dark eyes and black-tipped ears. The color change aids in camouflage as the snows of winter arrive. The snowshoe hare is primarily nocturnal and solitary. It feeds on herbs and grasses in summer, and branches and bark in winter, but will also eat meat if available.

Black-tailed Jackrabbit, *Lepus californicus*
Family Leporidae (Rabbits and Hares)
Size: ~23" long
Range: Low elevations of Colorado
Habitat: Prairies, open sage land, meadows

The black-tailed jackrabbit is a large, lanky hare with relatively long legs and huge, black-tipped ears. The color is gray brown, paler underneath, with a white tail that has a black stripe on top that extends onto the rump. The similar white-tailed jackrabbit has no dark upper surface on the tail and inhabits the mountains of eastern California. Jackrabbits are mostly nocturnal and solitary, highly alert, and able to elude predators with exceptionally fast runs and high jumps. They forage on grass and other vegetation, but may be limited to bark and buds in winter.

Desert Cottontail, *Sylvilagus audubonii*
Family Leporidae (Rabbits and Hares)
Size: 13" long
Range: Throughout Colorado
Habitat: Thickets, upland fields, dry brushy areas

The desert cottontail is relatively small, colored golden-gray with a pale reddish-brown patch on the back of its neck, a short, rounded, white tail (hence the common name), and long ears. Its eyes are quite large, and the rear feet are long and powerful. The cottontails' high rate of reproduction and general abundance make them an important food source for carnivorous wildlife. Desert cottontails are mostly nocturnal, but can be seen feeding at almost any time for grasses, herbs, branches, and bark. The rabbits never stray too far from brushy cover or their burrows. They are nearly identical to eastern cottontails but are a bit smaller with proportionately larger ears.

Eastern Cottontail, *Sylvilagus floridanus*
Family Leporidae (Rabbits and Hares)
Size: 15" long
Range: Eastern Colorado
Habitat: Open woodlands, areas near water, dense brush

Almost identical to the Desert Cottontail but a bit larger with proportionately smaller ears and found primarily in the eastern part of the state. The eastern cottontail is colored gray brown to reddish brown, with a short, rounded, white tail (hence the common name).. Its eyes are quite large, and its rear feet are long and powerful. Like other rabbits, they are an important food source for most carnivorous wildlife. Eastern cottontails are mostly nocturnal, but can be seen feeding at almost any time for grasses, herbs, branches, and bark. They never stay too far from brushy cover or their burrows.

Northern Flying Squirrel, *Glaucomys sabrinus*
Family Sciuridae (Squirrels)
Size: 16" with tail
Range: Northwestern Colorado
Habitat: Coniferous or deciduous woodlands, oak stands

The northern flying squirrel is small and unusual, designed to glide (not fly) from tree to tree or from tree to ground. Flaps of skin connect the front and rear feet; when outstretched, these flaps allow the squirrel to glide more than 100 feet and make a delicate landing. The color is grayish brown, darker along the flanks, and whitish below. These squirrels are active at night and are highly social, with several individuals sometimes sharing a nest site in a tree cavity or external structure. They forage for nuts, fruit, insects, fungus, and eggs, and store food in tree cavities for winter use.

Yellow-bellied Marmot, *Marmota flaviventris*
Family Sciuridae (Squirrels)
Size: ~24" long with tail (males larger than females)
Range: Mountainous central and western Colorado
Habitat: Rocky slopes and in boulders at high elevations

The yellow-bellied marmot is a heavy, roundish ground squirrel with small ears and a somewhat bushy tail of medium length. Its thick fur is pale tan-brown overall, with a yellowish belly and pale patches on the front of its face. Found alone or in groups, the marmot is active during the day, perching atop boulders or foraging for herbs, grasses, and seeds. It is often seen at the highest mountain summits, and undertakes a long winter hibernation in an underground burrow.

Golden-mantled Ground Squirrel, *Spermophilus lateralis*
Family Sciuridae (Squirrels)
Size: ~10" long with tail
Range: Mountainous central and western Colorado
Habitat: Open coniferous forest, campgrounds

The golden-mantled ground squirrel is one of many types of ground squirrels, all primarily ground-dwelling and able to stand upright on their hind legs with ease. It is shaped somewhat like a chipmunk, with a similar set of lateral, black-and-white stripes along the sides, but it has no head stripes. The overall color is golden-red on the front quarters and grayer on the back and tail, with whitish eye rings. The golden-mantled ground squirrel is more solitary than other ground squirrels, and most active during the day. It uses a burrow system to nest and store food, which includes nuts, berries, insects, and eggs. It hibernates for most of the winter.

Black-tailed Prairie Dog, *Cynomys ludovicianus*
Family Sciuridae (Squirrels)
Size: ~15" long with tail
Range: Central and eastern Colorado
Habitat: Arid prairie regions

The black-tailed prairie dog is a large, plump ground squirrel able to stand upright on its hind legs with ease. Its color is pale yellow or buff overall, with a black-tipped tail. It has small ears, a short tail, and substantial claws for digging. Diurnal and highly social, prairie dogs create vast burrow systems and mounds in a colony known as a "town." A sentinel individual usually perches atop a mound, alerting the colony of danger with a doglike bark. Prairie dogs feed on plant matter and insects, and do not undergo a true hibernation.

Eastern Fox Squirrel, *Sciurus niger*
Family Sciuridae (Squirrels)
Size: 24–30" long with tail
Range: Eastern Colorado
Habitat: Open, mature woodlands

The eastern fox squirrel is a large tree squirrel with a long, bushy tail. It occurs in variable color morphs: The body can be rusty brown to grayish to all black above, with the underside whitish or tawny. In Colorado the fox squirrel is usually reddish-brown on the back and sides, and pale orange on the belly, face, and legs. Eastern fox squirrels are generally solitary, searching in trees or on the ground for nuts, buds, and berries. In the fall, nuts are cached in tree cavities or in large nests in the crotches of trees, which the squirrels construct from leaves.

Least Chipmunk, *Tamias minimus*
Family Sciuridae (Squirrels)
Size: ~8" with tail
Range: Throughout Colorado
Habitat: Arid, high-elevation open forests to lowland sagebrush and rocky areas

The smallest chipmunk in North America, but similar in body shape to other chipmunks, the least chipmunk has a small body, large head and eyes, and a long, bushy tail. The most obvious field marks are the white-and-dark brown stripes across the head and along the back. Much geographical variation exists, but typically the least chipmunk's sides are orange brown, the underparts are pale gray, and the tail is mottled in the body colors, often striped with black near the base. The chipmunk usually holds its tail in a vertical position when running. Least chipmunks are active during the day from spring to fall, busily collecting nuts, berries, grasses, and insects, using an extendable cheek pouch to carry extra food for storage. They nest in burrows, under logs, or in trees, and spend the winter in partial hibernation underground, where they periodically awaken to nibble on bits of cached food. These chipmunks often visit campsites for food and can be quite vocal, emitting a high-pitched *chip*. The similar Colorado chipmunk is larger, with longer stripes on the back.

Red Squirrel, *Tamiasciurus hudsonicus*
Family Sciuridae (Squirrels)
Size: ~12" long with tail
Range: Central and western Colorado
Habitat: Coniferous or mixed woodlands

The red squirrel, also known as the pine squirrel and the chicka-ree, is feisty, highly territorial, and is most at home in trees. It is relatively small, with a bushy tail and large eyes encircled with white. The color is reddish-brown above and white below, with a dark band in between. The squirrel may be somewhat paler in winter months. Red squirrels are primarily active during the day, and at all times of the year. They eat the nuts of pine and spruce cones, but will also eat berries, insects, and mushrooms.

Abert's Squirrel *Sciurus aberti*
Family Sciuridae (Squirrels)
Size: ~20" long with tail
Range: Mountainous central and southwestern Colorado
Habitat: High-elevation ponderosa or mixed coniferous forest

Also known as the tassel-eared squirrel for obvious reasons, the Abert's squirrel is found only in the southern Rocky Mountains and in the Grand Canyon region of Arizona. It is a distinctive tree squirrel with a broad tail and pronounced ear tufts (which may be lacking or reduced in winter months). The color varies, but is generally dark gray above, nearly black along the sides, and white below. The tail is either all white or two-toned, with white below and gray above. Some individuals in the northern reaches of the squirrel's range are nearly all black with a black belly. Active during the day, Abert's squirrels leap from limb to limb among primarily ponderosa pines, feeding on all parts of the trees including the bark, cones, buds, and attached fungus or parasitic plants.

American Beaver, *Castor canadensis*
Family Castoridae (Beavers)
Size: 28" body; 10" tail
Range: Throughout Colorado
Habitat: Ponds, lakes, streams with adjacent woodlands

Once nearly extirpated because of hunting and trapping for pelts, this largest of North American rodents now covers most of its original range. The beaver is heavy and compact, with webbed rear feet, large front incisors, and a long, dexterous, scaled, flattened tail. The color is dark brown. Beavers are known for cooperative construction of impressive dams and lodges made from trees they have felled. Their presence is often announced by loud tail slaps on the water. Mostly nocturnal, beavers eat the tender, inner bark of trees, as well as small branches and buds.

Ord's Kangaroo Rat, *Dipodomys ordii*
Family Heteromyidae (Pocket Mice, Kangaroo Mice, and Kangaroo Rats)
Size: ~ 4" body; 5.5" tail
Range: Throughout Colorado
Habitat: Lowland prairies and scrublands with sandy soils

One of several species of kangaroo rats across the arid west, the Ord's kangaroo rat occupies the largest range and is one of the smaller varieties. It is a compact rodent with a relatively large head, a long tail with a bushy distal portion, and oversize rear feet, akin to a kangaroo. Its color is buff to rusty brown, with white lateral stripes across the lower body and the middle of the tail. Mostly nocturnal and somewhat solitary, kangaroo rats spend the day in their burrows. They hop about, kangaroo-style, foraging for plants, seeds, and insects. They are well adapted to dry conditions, and receive most of the water they need through their food.

Eastern Wood Rat, *Neotoma floridana*
Family Cricetidae (New World Mice and Rats)
Size: 21" long with tail
Range: Eastern Colorado
Habitat: Grasslands, woodlands, rural buildings

The eastern wood rat is a chunky, large rodent with a squarish
head, large ears, and hairy tail that is usually slightly less long than
its body. The fur is grayish-brown above, and white below and on
the feet. Eastern wood rats are nocturnal, breed year-round, and
feed on plant matter and seeds, as well as fungi. They build house-
like nests of sticks and debris in crevices, burrows, or caves, which
offer protection and a place to cache food. They are members of
the "pack rat" group, known to collect bits of small metallic refuse.

Deer Mouse, *Peromyscus maniculatus*
Family Cricetidae (New World Mice and Rats)
Size: 4" body; 3" tail
Range: Throughout Colorado
Habitat: Highly variable: grasslands, woodlands, mountains, brushlands

The deer mouse is common and widespread. It occurs in a wide range of habitats, and can vary in size and color depending on region. The appearance is typical of the mice, with a small body, pointed snout, large, black eyes, and large ears. The tail is thin and varies in length, but is typically slightly shorter than the body. Color ranges from grayish to brown or orange-brown above, with a white underside and lower part of the face. The tail is dark above, sharply contrasting with white below. Deer mice are most commonly active during the night, emerging from daytime refuges of burrows or under rocks and stumps. They scamper along the ground, in brush, or in trees gathering nuts, fruits, grasses, and insects. They store extra food to eat during lean winter months in a hidden cache, since they do not hibernate.

Porcupine, *Erethizon dorsatum*
Family Erethizontidae (Porcupine)
Size: ~28" with tail
Range: Throughout Colorado
Habitat: Forests, thickets

The porcupine is a primarily arboreal, chunky, lackadaisical rodent with small limbs, a bushy tail, and thousands of pointed barbed quills, which serve as its only defense. Its color is dark brown to blackish. Found alone or in groups, the porcupine is mostly nocturnal but can be seen at all times of the day, especially perched in trees. Porcupines feed on all types of plant matter, including buds, branches, bark, roots, and leaves.

Coyote, *Canis latrans*
Family Canidae (Coyotes, Wolves, and Foxes)
Size: 4' with tail
Range: Throughout Colorado
Habitat: Open country, scrub, grasslands

The coyote is an intelligent and adaptable canid that has been able to survive in a wide variety of habitats and in spite of persecution by humans. It looks like an average-size dog, with a long, thin muzzle and pointed ears. The color can range from gray to light brown or reddish. It has a bushy tail that is held low or between the legs. Coyotes hunt alone or in small packs, primarily during the night. Their diet is varied, and they scavenge for anything edible, including rodents, rabbits, snakes, berries, insects, and carrion.

Gray Wolf, *Canis lupus*
Family Canidae (Coyotes, Wolves, and Foxes)
Size: ~ 4.5' body, without tail (males larger than females)
Range: Northern Rocky Mountains
Habitat: Forests

Also known as the timber wolf, the gray wolf was once found throughout the western United States, but is now restricted to small wilderness areas and is very rarely sighted in Colorado. It is the country's largest canid, and is colored in varying combinations of black, gray, reddish, or even white in the north. Wolves live and travel in packs, with a tight social structure, and hunt large game such as elk and caribou as well as small mammals (down to mouse-size). Territory and communication are conveyed through piercing howls and urine marks.

Gray Fox, *Urocyon cinereoargenteus*
Family Canidae (Coyotes, Wolves, and Foxes)
Size: 3' with tail
Range: Throughout Colorado
Habitat: Open woodlands, brush, suburban areas

The gray fox is a small, stealthy, nimble canid with a bushy tail and
the ability to climb trees using its short, curved, retractable claws.
Its fur is gray and white-speckled above, reddish along the sides
and legs, and there is a black streak down the back and tail, ending in a black tail tip. Its muzzle is thin and small, while its ears are
comparatively large. Gray foxes are mostly solitary and nocturnal,
and feed on a varied diet that includes rabbits, rodents, insects,
nuts, and fruit.

27

Red Fox, *Vulpes vulpes*
Family Canidae (Coyotes, Wolves, and Foxes)
Size: 38" with tail
Range: Throughout Colorado except for the southeastern region
Habitat: Open woodlands, fields, brushy areas; may approach urban centers

Like other foxes, the red fox is wily, secretive, adaptable, and dog-like. It has a small muzzle, large ears, and a bushy tail. It is rusty red above, white or gray below, with black "stockings" on its legs and a white-tipped tail. Color variations may include black or slate gray, and the fox may have a dark cross along the shoulders. Red foxes are solitary hunters and are most active at night or in the twilight hours, seeking the shelter of a den during the day. They feed on small mammals, insects, carrion, plants, and berries, sometimes performing a dramatic leaping pounce to catch rodents.

Kit Fox, *Vulpes macrotis*
Family Canidae (Coyotes, Wolves, and Foxes)
Size: 28" with tail
Range: Southwestern Colorado
Habitat: Sandy arid areas, prairies, sagebrush

Colorado's smallest canid, and the only one found in desert regions, the kit fox is diminutive (house cat-size), with comparatively large ears and a delicate face. Its color is pale reddish-brown mottled with gray above, and lighter below. The tail has a black tip. The kit fox is primarily nocturnal, hunting for small mammals, insects, and reptiles, but it will also take carrion if available. The fox retreats to a den or burrow during the day. Some consider the kit fox to be the same species as the slightly larger swift fox, which inhabits areas of northern and eastern Colorado. Hybrids of these two species also appear where their ranges overlap.

American Black Bear, *Ursus americanus*
Family Ursidae (Bears)
Size: 3' tall at the shoulder; 6' tall standing (males larger than females)
Range: Central and western Colorado
Habitat: Forests, mountain valleys, open range

Although the smallest bear in North America, the American black bear is still heavy (up to 600 pounds) and lumbering, with thick (but not humped) shoulders, short legs, and small ears and tail. There is variation across its range, but in Colorado its color is black or cinnamon brown, with a light brown muzzle and sometimes a white patch on the chest. Black bears feed mostly at night, covering large areas while foraging for plants, roots, berries, grubs, and occasionally small animals, fish, and carrion. The black bear is usually solitary, except in mating season or when in family units consisting of cubs and a mother. The bear spends most of the winter hibernating in a den, but can be aroused quickly.

Grizzly Bear, *Ursus arctos horribilis*
Family Ursidae (Bears)
Size: ~3.5' tall at shoulder; 7' long; and 9' tall when standing, up to 800 lbs
Range: Northern Rocky Mountains; extirpated from Colorado but may be reintroduced
Habitat: Remote, high mountains

The grizzly bear is a subspecies of the brown bear that once roamed most of western North America; grizzlies are now restricted to wilderness areas where they are protected by law. Grizzlies are large and powerful, with a distinctive hump above the shoulder blades and a rounded, "dished" face. The thick fur is brown to golden brown, tipped with silver that gives the bear a frosted, grizzled appearance. Grizzlies are mostly solitary but will congregate around food sources, like heavy runs of salmon, upon which they gorge. They also eat berries, plants, grubs, and mammals to the size of bison or moose. In the winter they undergo a light hibernation, or torpor.

Ringtail, *Bassariscus astutus*
Family Procyonidae (Ringtail and Raccoon)
Size: ~30" with tail
Range: Central and western Colorado
Habitat: Rocky deserts, forests

The ringtail is a small, secretive mammal with delicate features, big, dark eyes, and a long, bushy tail. Although sometimes referred to as the ringtail cat, it is not related to cats but allied more with raccoons. Its color is light brown above, paler below, with a striped black-and-white tail. Mostly nocturnal, it is usually found alone or in pairs. Ringtail are very agile climbers, using their long tails and flexible ankles to navigate through trees and rocks. They forage for both plants and animals, with a diet that includes berries, insects, birds, and small mammals.

Raccoon, *Procyon lotor*
Family Procyonidae (Ringtail and Raccoon)
Size: 34" with tail
Range: Lower elevations of Colorado
Habitat: Woodlands, streams or lakesides, urban areas

The raccoon is a highly adaptable mammal, equally at home in remote forests or urban centers. It is stocky and heavy, with a short, masked face and a bushy coat. Its color is pale gray mixed with black, with a tail ringed in black and gray. Incredibly dexterous fingers allow it to undo knots and even work doorknobs. Raccoon are primarily nocturnal and may be seen alone or in small groups. They prefer to feed near a water source, often dipping their food in water first, and will eat just about anything, including fruit, nuts, insects, fish, crayfish, and worms.

Northern River Otter, *Lontra canadensis*
Family Mustelidae (Weasels and Otters)
Size: 4' with tail
Range: Throughout Colorado
Habitat: Areas near streams, lakes, or estuaries

The river otter is a large, curious, and playful member of the weasel family with a mostly aquatic lifestyle. It is elongate and sinuous, with small ears, webbed feet, and a long, somewhat thickened tail to aid in swimming. Its fur is thick, dark brown above and pale gray below and across the lower face. River otters are social and often travel in small family groups. They hunt primarily in the water for fish, amphibians, or aquatic invertebrates. They live in burrows near water and form well-used trails along the shore or between water sources.

Marten, *Martes americana*
Family Mustelidae (Weasels and Otters)
Size: ~25" with tail
Range: Mountainous Colorado
Habitat: Forested areas

The marten is an elongate, slender mustelid with a long tail, short legs, and a pointed snout. It is stockier that a weasel, with larger, rounded ears, but is much smaller than a fisher, with whom it shares a similar range. Its color is golden brown, with a buff or orange patch on its throat and chest. Numbers of this species have been severely reduced by trappers for the luxurious pelt. Martens are nocturnal and solitary. Adept climbers, they hunt small mammals in trees or on the ground, and may also feed on nuts and berries when available.

Black-footed Ferret, *Mustela nigripes*
Family Mustelidae (Weasels and Otters)
Size: ~21" with tail; ~2.25 lbs
Range: Throughout Colorado
Habitat: Prairies

The black-footed ferret is a rare and endangered species whose populations have diminished due to the extermination of its favored food, the prairie dog. It is shaped like a large weasel, with an elongate body, long neck and tail, short legs, and small ears. It is colored pale golden brown, with black feet, a black tail tip, and a black facial mask. Ferrets are mostly nocturnal and solitary, and hunt prairie dogs by slinking into their burrows.

Long-tailed Weasel, *Mustela frenata*
Family Mustelidae (Weasels and Otters)
Size: 14" with tail
Range: Throughout Colorado
Habitat: Woodlands, fields with brushy cover, often found near water

The long-tailed weasel is a wily, small, elongate, long-necked predator, and one of Colorado's smallest meat eaters. It is reddish brown, buff-colored on its underparts and throat, and has a black tip on its long tail. It is nocturnal and solitary, an excellent climber, and, due to its thin, sinuous shape and short legs, the weasel can slip into burrows to attack rodents living within. Long-tailed weasels also hunt rabbits, birds, eggs, and fish. To den, they use the existing burrows of similar-size rodents.

American Mink, *Neovison vison*
Family Mustelidae (Weasels and Otters)
Size: 20" with tail
Range: Throughout Colorado
Habitat: Near streams and marshes

The American mink is an elongate, short-legged member of the weasel family with a long tail, webbed feet, and a semiaquatic lifestyle. Its luxurious pelt is dark blackish brown; minks sometimes have a whitish area around the mouth and may have pale spotting on their undersides. Minks are mostly nocturnal and solitary, are excellent swimmers, and never stray too far from a water source. They are carnivores, eating aquatic animals and invertebrates, but will also take birds, eggs, and rabbits.

Badger, *Taxidea taxus*
Family Mustelidae (Weasels and Otters)
Size: ~24" long with tail
Range: Throughout Colorado
Habitat: Grasslands, desert

The badger is a compact, tough mustelid with a short tail and very long claws, especially on its front feet. It is densely furred, and colored pale gray brown with a white or buff belly and black feet. It has a white stripe through its forehead that runs over its head, and a white-and-black patterned face. Badgers are solitary and nocturnal, though often visible during early morning hours. They use their strong clawed feet to excavate rodent burrows for the prey therein, and will also eat reptiles and birds. In cold climates badgers hibernate in underground burrows.

Striped Skunk, *Mephitis mephitis*
Family Mephitidae (Skunks)
Size: 22" with tail
Range: Throughout Colorado
Habitat: Woodlands, brush, suburban parks; usually near a water source

The striped skunk is known primarily for its ability to elude danger by spraying a noxious fluid from an anal duct. A stocky, weasel-like mammal, it has a long, bushy tail and long front claws for digging. Its color is black, with broad white stripes running down its sides that merge into a white stripe on the upper part of the tail. Usually solitary, striped skunks stay in dens during the day and forage at night. Being omnivorous, they eat a wide variety of foods including fruit, nuts, insects, small mammals, and eggs.

Western Spotted Skunk, *Spilogale gracilis*
Family Mephitidae (Skunks)
Size: 18" with tail
Range: Throughout Colorado
Habitat: Brushy open woodlands, coastal scrub, grasslands; usually near a
water source

The western spotted skunk is smaller than the striped skunk but
shares its defensive ability to spray a noxious liquid from ducts
near its anus. It is weasel-like, with fine, soft fur, a thick, bushy tail,
and long claws. Its color is black, with variable and irregular white
spotting and striping on its head and back, and a white-tipped
tail. Solitary and nocturnal, these skunks stay in dens during the
day. They can climb trees but mostly forage on the ground, eating
a variety of foods including fruit, insects, small mammals, birds,
and eggs.

Mountain Lion, *Puma concolor*
Family Felidae (Cats)
Size: 7' body; 2.5' tail (males larger than females)
Range: Central and western Colorado
Habitat: Open to dense woodlands, brush

The mountain lion (also known as the cougar or puma) is a huge (about 125 pounds), reclusive, powerful cat. It has a long tail, and its fur is a blend of tawny browns, tans, and grays, paler on the underside and white on the chest and throat. The tail tip is dark brown, as are the backs of the ears and marks on the muzzle. Mountain lions are mostly solitary, except during breeding season or when mothers are with kittens. They hunt by stealth, waiting on rocky ledges or in trees for prey to pass, or slinking through grass to ambush prey, which includes deer, elk, and smaller mammals.

Bobcat, *Lynx rufus*
Family Felidae (Cats)
Size: 28" body; 5" tail
Range: Throughout Colorado
Habitat: A wide variety of habitats including forests, riparian areas, scrub

The bobcat is about double the size of a housecat, is well cam-ouflaged, and has a very short, "bobbed" tail. Its face appears wide due to long fur tufts below its ears, and the ears are tipped with short, black hairs. The color is light brown to reddish above, pale or whitish below, and spotted with dark brown or black that sometimes is streaked on the animal's legs. The tail is striped and black along the top edge. Bobcats are typically active during the early morning and after dusk; in winter they are active during the day. They hunt by stealth, ambushing their favored prey of rabbits, other small mammals, and birds. The similar lynx is a bit larger, and has an all-black tail.

Pronghorn, *Antilocapra americana*
Family Antilocapridae (Pronghorn)
Size: 4.5' body (males larger than females)
Range: Throughout Colorado
Habitat: Grassy plains, sagebrush

The pronghorn is the only member of its family, and bears a resemblance to the antelopes of the Old World. It is light brown with a white rump patch, belly, and band about the neck. The neck also has a darker brown band and dark facial patterning. Both sexes have rough, black, flattened horns, which curve at the tip and have a single, forward-projecting prong. The outer sheath of the horn is shed and regrown each year. Pronghorns are primarily active during the morning and afternoon, are found singly or in small groups, and forage on grasses, herbaceous plants, and sagebrush. When pursued they can run up to 40 mph, making them the fastest mammals in North America.

Bison, *Bison bison*
Family Bovidae (Sheep, Goats, and Bison)
Size: ~ 6' tall at shoulder; 8' body (males larger than females)
Range: Isolated regions of western and northeastern Colorado
Habitat: Grassy plains, open woodlands

The largest land mammal in North America (weighing up to 1,200 pounds or more), the bison is a massive bovid that once roamed huge expanses of the continent but is now limited to small protected areas. Both sexes have humped backs and large heads with curving horns. The color is brownish, with a thick, shaggy, darker head and forequarters. Bison are fast runners for their size, are active during the day, and are gregarious. They form large grazing herds, eating mostly grasses and sedges, and spend much of the day wallowing or chewing their cud.

Bighorn Sheep, *Ovis canadensis*
Family Bovidae (Sheep, Goats, and Bison)
Size: ~ 3' tall at shoulder; 6' body (males larger than females)
Range: Central and western Colorado
Habitat: Rugged, mountainous areas

The bighorn sheep is the largest of the true sheep, and includes subspecies found in the Rocky Mountains, the Sierra Nevada, and the desert Southwest. They are closely related to the dall sheep of Alaska and western Canada, but have larger horns. The bighorn is stocky, with a strong neck and shoulders, and is colored light brown to grayish with a white rump and white backs of the legs. Both sexes have horns, but those of the male are much larger, curve in an arc to the back, and can weigh up to 25 pounds. The horns are used in dramatic head-butting rituals during the mating season. Sure-footed and agile, bighorn sheep form groups. They forage on all varieties of plants and tree branches, and are able to eat very dry and tough material.

Mountain Goat, *Oreamnos americanus*
Family Bovidae (Sheep, Goats, and Bison)
Size: ~ 3' tall at shoulder (males larger than females)
Range: Colorado's northern Rocky Mountains
Habitat: Cliffs at high altitudes, near or above timberline

Found only in North America, the mountain goat, also known as the Rocky Mountain goat, is a stocky, sure-footed member of the bovid family, and the largest mammal likely to be seen in the alpine zone. It is all white or cream-colored, with dense, wooly fur and a shaggy beard below the throat. The hooves and thin, backward-curving horns are black. Horns are present in both males and females. The shoulder is humped, and the tail is short and stubby. Able to withstand extreme cold, mountain goats are seen singly or in small groups foraging on impossibly steep, rocky slopes for lichens, grasses, herbs, ferns, and tree branches.

Elk, *Cervus elaphus*
Family Cervidae (Deer, Elk, and Moose)
Size: 8' body; 5" tail (males larger than females)
Range: Throughout Colorado's mountains
Habitat: Mountainous forests, high meadows

The elk, also known as wapiti, is a large, gregarious member of the deer family. Its fur is short in the summer, longer in the winter, and colored pale rusty brown, with a darker neck and face. The rump is buff, surrounded by dark brown, with a pale, stubby tail. Males have a shaggy, dark mane about the neck, and large antlers with tines growing from a central beam. Usually active in the morning and evening, elk form large herds, sometimes numbering hundreds of individuals. They browse for grass, herbs, branches, and the tender inner bark of trees.

Mule Deer, *Odocoileus hemionus*
Family Cervidae (Deer, Elk, and Moose)
Size: 6' long with tail (males larger than females)
Range: Throughout Colorado
Habitat: Quite variable; forests, chaparral, bushy grasslands

The mule deer is quite common throughout its range, and so-called because of its very large, mulelike ears. Its color is gray brown in winter, rusty brown in summer, with a white throat, muzzle, and belly. Depending on the region, its tail may have a black tip or may have black on the top surface. Males have antlers that are evenly forked (not with tines from a central beam, as in the white-tailed deer). In summer, the antlers are covered in velvet. Mule deer are active at twilight, moving in small groups or singly, and browsing for tree branches, grasses, and herbs.

White-tailed Deer, *Odocoileus virginianus*
Family Cervidae (Deer, Elk, and Moose)
Size: 6' body; 10" tail
Range: Eastern and northwestern Colorado
Habitat: Dense forest, forest edges

North America's smallest deer, the white-tailed deer is a secretive mammal of thick forests. It is very agile, fast, and able to outmaneuver most predators. The male has antlers with a main beam that supports smaller prongs. The color of its fur is reddish brown, with a white belly and throat. When alarmed, the white-tailed deer raises its tail, revealing the brilliant white underside, hence its colloquial name of "flagtail." White-tailed deer travel in small groups in summer, but in winter may congregate in larger herds. Being herbivores, they forage for grasses, herbs, and nuts.

Moose, *Alces alces*
Family Cervidae (Deer, Elk, and Moose)
Size: ~8.5' body (males larger than females)
Range: Northwestern Colorado
Habitat: Moist or marshy woodlands

The moose is the largest member of the deer family (weighing up to 800 pounds or more), and is second only to the bison in size among North American mammals. It has long, thin legs, a broad, drooping snout, and a hanging tuft of hair below the throat called a "bell." Males have huge, palmate antlers that grow to five feet across. The color is brown overall, with pale gray legs. Usually found alone or in small family groups, moose are herbivores that graze on woody twigs and branches, and aquatic plants.

BIRDS:
NONPASSERINES

Canada Goose, *Branta canadensis*
Family Anatidae (Geese, Ducks, and Mergansers)
Size: 27–35" depending on race
Season: Winter; during spring and fall migrations
Habitat: Marshes, grasslands, public parks, golf courses

The Canada goose is the state's most common goose, and is found in suburban settings. It is vegetarian, foraging on land for grass, seeds, and grain or in the water by upending like the dabbling ducks. It has a heavy body with short, thick legs and a long neck. Overall, its coloring is barred gray brown, with a white rear, a short black tail, a black neck, and a white patch running from under the neck to behind the eye. During its powerful flight the goose's white rump makes a semicircular patch between the tail and back. Its voice is a loud *honk.* In flight Canada geese form the classic V formation. The adult is illustrated.

Snow Goose, *Chen caerulescens*
Family Anatidae (Geese, Ducks, and Mergansers)
Size: 28"
Season: During spring and fall migration
Habitat: Grasslands, marshes

The snow goose forms huge, impressive flocks when it visits Colorado during spring and fall migrations between the arctic tundra and southern North America and Mexico. It has two color forms: the "blue" and the more common "white." The white form is predominantly white, with black outer wing feathers and a pale yellowish wash to the face during summer. The blue form retains the white head and lower belly but is otherwise dark slate gray or brownish gray. In both morphs, its bill is thick at the base, pink, and has a black patch where the mandibles meet. The legs of both morphs are pink. Snow geese feed mostly on the ground, consuming shoots, roots, grains, and insects. The similar Ross's goose is smaller, with a shorter bill. The white morph adult is illustrated.

Mallard, *Anas platyrhynchos*
Family Anatidae (Geese, Ducks, and Mergansers)
Size: 23"
Season: Year-round
Habitat: Parks and urban areas; virtually any environment with water

The ubiquitous mallard is the most abundant duck in the Northern Hemisphere. It is a classic dabbling duck, plunging its head into the water with its tail up, searching for aquatic plants, animals, and snails. It will also eat worms, seeds, insects, and even mice. Noisy and quacking, it is heavy but a strong flier. The male has a dark head with green or blue iridescence, a white neck ring, and a large yellow bill. His underparts are pale, with a chestnut brown breast. The female is plain brownish, with buff-colored, scalloped markings. She also has a dark eye line and an orangey bill with a dark center. The speculum is blue on both sexes, and the tail coverts often curl upward. Mallards form huge floating flocks called "rafts." To achieve flight, the mallard lifts straight into the air without running. The breeding male, below, and a female, above, are illustrated.

Northern Pintail, *Anas acuta*
Family Anatidae (Geese, Ducks, and Mergansers)
Size: 21"
Season: Year-round
Habitat: Marshes, shallow lakes

Among the most abundant ducks in North America, the northern pintail is an elegant, slender, dabbling duck with a long neck, small head, and narrow wings. In breeding plumage the male has long, pointed, central tail feathers. He is gray along his back and sides, with a brown head and a white breast. A white stripe extends from the breast along the back of the neck. The female is mottled brown-and-tan overall, with a light brown head. To feed, the northern pintail bobs its head into the water to capture aquatic invertebrates and plants from the muddy bottom. It rises directly out of the water to take flight. The breeding male, below, and a female, above, are illustrated.

Common Merganser, *Mergus merganser*
Family Anatidae (Geese, Ducks, and Mergansers)
Size: 25"
Season: Year-round, but most often in winter
Habitat: Lakes, rivers

The common merganser is a long, sleek, diving duck with a rounded head and a long, thin bill. The breeding male is dark gray above and white (sometimes washed with pale brown) below. His head is black with a metallic green sheen, and the bill is red with a dark tip. The female looks similar to the nonbreeding male, gray overall with a rusty-brown head and a white chin and neck. Also known as the sawtooth, the common merganser dives for fish or aquatic invertebrates, and grips its prey with the sawlike serrations on its bill. It runs across the water to take off, and its flight is fast and direct. The breeding male, below, and a female, above, are illustrated.

Ruddy Duck, *Oxyura jamaicensis*
Family Anatidae (Geese, Ducks, and Mergansers)
Size: 15"
Season: Summer
Habitat: Open water, wetlands

The ruddy duck is a "stiff-tailed duck," part of a group known for rigid tail feathers that are often cocked up in display. It dives deep for its food, which consists of aquatic vegetation, and flies low over the water with quick wing beats. A relatively small duck, with a big head and a flat, broad body, the breeding male is a rich sienna brown overall, with white cheeks, a black cap and nape, and a bright blue bill. The female is drab, with a conspicuous dark stripe across her cheek. Nonbreeding males become gray. The ruddy duck can sink low into the water, grebelike, and will often dive to escape danger. The breeding male, below, and a female, above, are illustrated.

Ring-necked Pheasant, *Phasianus colchicus*
Family Phasianidae (Pheasants, Grouse, and Turkeys)
Size: 21" (male) 34" (female)
Season: Year-round
Habitat: Grasslands, woodland edges, agricultural land with brushy cover

The ring-necked pheasant is a large, chicken-shaped bird with a long, pointed tail. The male is ornately patterned in rufous tones, gold, and blue gray, with pale spotting on the wings and back and dark spotting underneath. His head is an iridescent green blue with a tufted crown; he has red facial skin and a white ring about the neck. The female is mottled brown above and plain below, without obvious head markings. Ring-necked pheasants peck on the ground for seeds, grasses, and insects. Its vocalizations include a harsh *auk* caw, and muffled wing fluttering. The adult male is illustrated.

Dusky Grouse, *Dendragapus obscurus*
Family Phasianidae (Pheasants, Grouse, and Turkeys)
Size: 19"; males larger than females
Season: Year-round
Habitat: Forest edges, open brushland, mountain ridges

The dusky grouse of the interior was once considered a blue grouse, the same species as the Pacific region's sooty grouse. It is large and heavy, with a long tail and thick, feathered legs. The male is finely marked gray-brown overall, with some white patterning along the back, wings, and sides. He has a relatively thick bill and an orange-red comb above his eye. In display he spreads his neck feathers to reveal a circle of white feathers around a bare patch of reddish skin. The female is extensively mottled gray, brown, and white overall. The dusky grouse forages on the ground for seeds, berries, and insects, and voices a deep, soft, resonant *yoop, yoop.* Strangely, the grouse move from low elevations in summer to higher elevations in the winter. The adult male is illustrated.

White-tailed Ptarmigan, *Lagopus leucura*
Family Phasianidae (Pheasants, Grouse, and Turkeys)
Size: 13"; males larger than females
Season: Year-round
Habitat: High elevations in treeless, mountainous areas; tundra zones

The white-tailed ptarmigan is small, chunky, and grouselike, with a small head and bill. The breeding male is white below with dark spotting on the breast and sides, and mottled brown above and on the central tail area. A red comb is above the eye. Nonbreeding adults of both sexes are all white except for black eyes and bills. The breeding female is mottled brown overall, but has white wings and corners on her tail. The ptarmigan's legs and toes are feathered for arctic conditions. White-tailed ptarmigans forage on the ground for plant buds, insects, and berries. The breeding male, below, and the nonbreeding male, above, are illustrated.

Greater Sage-grouse, *Centrocercus urophasianus*
Family Phasianidae (Pheasants, Grouse, and Turkeys)
Size: 28"; males larger than females
Season: Year-round
Habitat: Open sagebrush country

The greater sage-grouse is Colorado's largest grouse. It is a heavy bird with a relatively small head and a long, pointed tail. The male is well camouflaged: mottled gray-brown on the back, with a clean, white breast and a black belly. He has a black throat and white streaking along his neck, and a sage green comb above the eyes. The female is mottled gray-brown overall, with a plainer head, but she retains the black belly. The male engages in a dramatic display during courtship, with his tail spread and raised and his breast feathers spread to reveal two yellow air sacs. The air sacs produce a low *gloop* or hooting noise. Grouse feed almost exclusively on sagebrush. The adult male is illustrated.

Wild Turkey, *Meleagris gallopavo*
Family Phasianidae (Pheasants, Grouse, and Turkeys)
Size: 36–48"; males larger than females
Season: Year-round
Habitat: Open mixed woodlands

The wild turkey is a very large, dark, ground-dwelling bird (but is slimmer than the domestic turkey). The head and neck appear small for the body size, and the legs are thick and stout. The heavily barred plumage is quite iridescent in strong light. The turkey's head and neck are covered with bluish, warty, crinkled bare skin that droops under the chin in a red wattle. Often foraging in flocks, wild turkeys search the ground for seeds, grubs, and insects, then roost at night in trees. Males emit the familiar *gobble,* while females are less vocal, making a soft clucking sound. In display the male hunches with his tail up and spread like a giant fan. Southwestern races, which are seen in Colorado, show white banding on the tail. The adult male is illustrated.

Pied-billed Grebe, *Podilymbus podiceps*
Family Podicipedidae (Grebes)
Size: 13"
Season: Year-round in southern Colorado; summer in northern Colorado
Habitat: Freshwater ponds and lakes

The pied-billed grebe is small and secretive. It lurks in sheltered waters, diving for small fish, leeches, snails, and crawfish. When alarmed, or to avoid predatory snakes and hawks, it sinks below the surface until only its head is above water. It is brownish overall but slightly darker above, with a tiny tail and short wings. Breeding adults have a conspicuous dark ring around the middle of the bill. The ring is missing in winter plumage. The grebe nests on a floating mat of vegetation. The breeding adult is illustrated.

Double-crested Cormorant, *Phalacrocorax auritus*
Family Phalacrocoracidae (Cormorants)
Size: 32"
Season: Summer; during spring and fall migrations
Habitat: Open water

Named for the two long, white plumes that emerge from behind its eyes during breeding season, the double-crested cormorant is an expert swimmer that dives underwater to chase down fish. Because its plumage lacks the normal oils to repel water, the cormorant will stand with wings outstretched to dry itself. The double-crested cormorant is solid black with a pale glossy cast on its back and wings. The eye is bright green, the bill is thin and hooked, and the throat patch and lores are yellow. The breeding adult is illustrated.

American White Pelican, *Pelecanus erythrorhynchos*
Family Pelecanidae (Pelicans)
Size: 62"
Season: Spring and fall migrations
Habitat: Open freshwater lakes and rivers

One of North America's largest birds, the American white pelican has a wingspan of more than 9 feet. It is white overall, with black flight feathers. The massive bill is orange, with a membranous, expandable throat pouch. In posture the pelican holds its neck in a characteristic strong kink and its folded wings in a peak along its back. It often feeds in cooperative groups, herding fish as they swim and scooping them up by dipping their bills in the water. The white pelican never plunge-dives like the brown pelican. When breeding, a strange horny growth appears on the upper mandible in both sexes. The nonbreeding adult is illustrated.

Great Blue Heron, *Ardea herodias*
Family Ardeidae (Herons and Egrets)
Size: 46"
Season: Year-round
Habitat: Most aquatic areas, including lakes, creeks, and marshes

The great blue heron is the largest heron in North America. Walking slowly through shallow water or fields, it stalks fish, crabs, and small vertebrates, catching them with its massive bill. With long legs and a long neck, the heron is blue-gray overall, with a white face and a heavy yellow-orange bill. Its crown is black, and supports plumes of medium length. The front of the neck is white, with distinct black chevrons fading into breast plumes. In flight the neck is tucked back, and the heron's wing beats are regular and labored. The adult is illustrated.

67

Turkey Vulture, *Cathartes aura*
Family Cathartidae (New World Vultures)
Size: 27"
Season: Summer
Habitat: Open, dry country

The turkey vulture is known for its effortless, skilled soaring. It will often soar for hours, without flapping, rocking in the breeze on 6-foot wings that form an upright V shape, or dihedral angle. The vulture has a black body and inner wing, with pale flight feathers and pale tail feathers that give it a noticeable two-toned appearance from below. The tail is longish, and the feet extend no more than halfway past the base of the tail. The head is naked, red, and small, so the bird appears almost headless in flight. The bill is strongly hooked to aid in tearing apart the vulture's favored food—carrion. Juveniles have a dark gray head. Turkey vultures often roost in flocks and form groups around food or at a roadkill site. The adult is illustrated.

Northern Harrier, *Circus cyaneus*
Family Accipitridae (Hawks and Eagles)
Size: 18"; females larger than males
Season: Year-round
Habitat: Open fields, wetlands

Also known as the marsh hawk, the northern harrier flies low over the landscape, methodically surveying its hunting grounds for rodents and other small animals. When it spots prey, aided by its acute hearing, it will drop abruptly to the ground to attack. The northern harrier is a thin raptor with a long tail and long, flame-shaped wings that are broad in the middle. The face has a distinct owl-like facial disk, and there is a conspicuous white patch at the rump. Males are gray above, with a white, streaked breast and black wing tips. Females are brown with a barred breast. The juvenile is similar in plumage to the female, but with a pale belly. The female, below, and a male, above, are illustrated.

Sharp-shinned Hawk, *Accipiter striatus*
Family Accipitridae (Hawks and Eagles)
Size: 10–14"; females larger than males
Season: Year-round
Habitat: Woodlands, bushy areas

The sharp-shinned hawk is Colorado's smallest accipiter, with a longish, squared tail and stubby, rounded wings. Its short wings allow for agile flight in tight, wooded quarters, where it quickly attacks small birds in flight. It is grayish above and light below, barred with pale rufous stripes. The eyes are set forward on the face to aid in the direct pursuit of prey. The juvenile is white below, streaked with brown. The sharp-shinned hawk may be confused with the larger Cooper's hawk. The adult is illustrated.

Red-tailed Hawk, *Buteo jamaicensis*
Family Accipitridae (Hawks and Eagles)
Size: 20"
Season: Year-round
Habitat: Prairies, open country

This widespread species is the most common buteo in the United States. It has broad, rounded wings and a stout, hooked bill. Its plumage is highly variable depending on geographic location. In general, the underparts are light, with darker streaking that forms a dark band across the belly, the upperparts are dark brown, and the tail is rufous. Light spotting occurs along the scapulars. In flight there is a noticeable dark patch along the inner leading edge of the underwing. Red-tailed hawks glide down from perches, such as telephone poles and posts in open country, to catch rodents. They also may hover to spot prey. They are usually seen alone or in pairs. The voice is the familiar *keeer!* The western adult is illustrated.

Ferruginous Hawk, *Buteo regalis*
Family Accipitridae (Hawks and Eagles)
Size: 23"; females larger than males
Season: Year-round
Habitat: Dry prairies, open country

The ferruginous hawk is Colorado's largest buteo. It has a thick body and neck, a large, hooked bill, and long, broad wings. Two color morphs occur: light and dark. The light morph is white below, with rufous barring on the flanks and thighs; the back is mottled brown and rufous, with grayish flight feathers. The dark morph is dark brown overall, with white on the undersides of the flight feathers and tail. Ferruginous hawks stalk prey—small mammals—from perches, or by hovering or soaring. The light morph adult is illustrated.

Bald Eagle, *Haliaeetus leucocephalus*
Family Accipitridae (Hawks and Eagles)
Size: 30–40"; females larger than males
Season: Year-round; during winter
Habitat: Lakes and rivers with tall perches or cliffs

The bald eagle is a large raptor that is fairly uncommon even though its range is widespread. It eats fish or scavenges dead animals, and congregates in large numbers where food is abundant. Plumage is dark brown, which contrasts with its white head and tail. Juveniles show white splotching across the wings and breast. The yellow bill is large and powerful, and the talons are large and sharp. In flight the bald eagle holds its wings fairly flat and straight, resembling a long plank. Bald eagles make huge nests of sticks high in trees. The adult is illustrated.

American Kestrel, *Falco sparverius*
Family Falconidae (Falcons)
Size: 10"
Season: Year-round
Habitat: Open country, urban areas

Colorado's most common falcon, the American kestrel is tiny (robin-size), with long, pointed wings and tail, and fast flight. It hovers above fields or dives from a perch in branches or on a wire to capture small animals and insects. The kestrel's upperparts are rufous and barred with black, its wings are blue gray, and its breast is buff or white and streaked with black spots. The head is patterned with a gray crown and vertical patches of black down the face. The female has rufous wings and a barred tail. Also known as the sparrow hawk, the kestrel has a habit of flicking its tail up and down while perched. The adult male is illustrated.

Prairie Falcon, *Falco mexicanus*
Family Falconidae (Falcons)
Size: 17"; females larger than males
Season: Year-round
Habitat: Prairies, open land near cliffs and mountains

The prairie falcon is large, with a long tail and narrow, pointed wings. The body is pale brown gray above, and white with brown streaking below. The head is patterned with a white ear patch and chin and a dark malar patch. The falcon has large, black eyes. The underside, as seen in flight, is marked with dark inner wing coverts and axillar (armpit) feathers. Prairie falcons attack small animals on the ground from a perch or after aerial pursuit. The adult is illustrated.

Sandhill Crane, *Grus canadensis*
Family Gruidae (Cranes)
Size: 45"
Season: Spring and fall during migration
Habitat: Fields, shallow wetlands

The sandhill crane is tall, with long, strong legs, a long neck, and a long, straight bill. The long, thick tertial feathers create the distinctive bustle found on the rears of all cranes. The top of the sandhill crane's head is covered by red, bare skin. Plumage is gray overall, but may become spotted with rust-colored stains caused by preening with a bill stained by iron-rich mud. Flocks of cranes graze in fields, gleaning grains, insects, and small animals, then return to roost in protected wetland areas. The voice of the sandhill crane is a throaty, penetrating, trumpeting sound. Unlike a heron, the crane flies in groups with its neck extended. The adult is illustrated.

Killdeer, *Charadrius vociferus*
Family Charadriidae (Plovers)
Size: 10"
Season: Summer
Habitat: Fields, farmlands, lakeshores, meadows

The killdeer gets its name from its piercing *kill-dee* call, which is often heard before these well-camouflaged plovers are seen. Well adapted to human-altered environments, the killdeer is quite widespread and gregarious. It has long, pointed wings, a long tail, and a conspicuous double-banded breast. Its upper parts are dark brown, its belly is white, and its head is patterned with a white supercilium and forehead. The tail is rusty orange with a black tip. In flight a noticeable white stripe can be seen across the flight feathers. The killdeer is known for its classic "broken wing" display, which it uses to distract predators from its nest and young. The adult is illustrated.

American Avocet, *Recurvirostra americana*
Family Recurvirostridae (Avocets and Stilts)
Size: 18"
Season: Summer
Habitat: Shallow wetlands, marshes

The elegant American avocet has a long, delicate, black, upturned bill and long, thin, blue-gray legs. The upperparts are patterned black and white, the belly is white, and the head and neck are light orange-brown, the face punctuated with black eyes. The bill of the female is slightly shorter than that of the male, with a greater bend. Nonbreeding adults have a pale gray head and neck. Avocets use a side-to-side sweeping motion with their bills to stir up small crustaceans and insect larvae as they wade methodically through the shallows. They may even submerge their heads as the water deepens. They are adept swimmers and emit a *wheet!* call in alarm. The breeding male, below, and a female, above, are illustrated.

Greater Yellowlegs, *Tringa melanoleuca*
Family Scolopacidae (Sandpipers and Phalaropes)
Size: 14"
Season: Summer
Habitat: Marshes

The greater yellowlegs is sometimes called the "telltale" bird, as the sentinel of a flock raises an alarm when danger is near, flying off and circling to return. The bird has long, bright yellow legs, a long neck, a dark, slightly upturned bill, and a white eye ring. The upperparts are dark gray and mottled, while the underparts are white, with barring on the flanks. In breeding plumage the barring is noticeably darker and more extensive. To feed, the greater yellowlegs strides forward actively to pick small aquatic prey from the water or to chase fish. The lesser yellowlegs is similar in appearance, but smaller. The nonbreeding adult is illustrated.

79

Spotted Sandpiper, *Actitis macularius*
Family Scolopacidae (Sandpipers and Phalaropes)
Size: 7.5"
Season: Summer
Habitat: Creeksides, edges of lakes and ponds

The solitary spotted sandpiper is known for its exaggerated, constant, bobbing motion. It has a compact body, a long tail, and a
short neck and legs. Plumage is brown above and light below,
with a white shoulder patch. It has a white eye ring and superciliary stripe above the dark eye line. In breeding plumage the spotted sandpiper develops heavy spotting from its chin to its lower
flanks and barring on the back. Its bill is orange with a dark tip.
It has short wings, and in flight a thin white stripe on the upper
wing is visible. To forage, the sandpiper teeters about, picking
small prey from the water and insects from along the shoreline.
The breeding male is illustrated.

California Gull, *Larus californicus*
Family Laridae (Gulls and Terns)
Size: 21"
Season: Summer; transient in spring and fall
Habitat: Lakes, rivers, prairie wetlands

The California gull is medium-size, with a relatively thin, long bill. The breeding adult is medium blue-gray above and white below, with white edges to the tertials and secondaries. The primaries are black with white spotting, and the tail is white. The head is rounded, the eyes are dark, and the bill is yellow orange, with a black-and-red spot near the tip. The legs are greenish yellow. In winter adults show brownish streaking on the nape. California gulls breed in large colonies, and feed on a variety of food including fish, small mammals, and insects. The gull's voice is a harsh *squawk*. The breeding adult is illustrated.

Rock Pigeon, *Columba livia*
Family Columbidae (Pigeons and Doves)
Size: 12"
Season: Year-round
Habitat: Urban areas, farmland

The rock pigeon, formerly known as the rock dove, is common, seen in almost every urban area across the continent. Introduced from Europe, where they inhabit rocky cliffs, rock doves have adapted to city life, and domestication has resulted in a huge variety of plumage colors and patterns. The original, wild version is a stocky gray bird with a darker head and neck, and green to purple iridescence along the sides of the neck. The eye is bright red, and the bill has a fleshy, white cere at the base of the upper mandible. Two dark bars can be seen across the dove's back when the wing is folded, the rump is white, and the tail has a dark terminal band. Variants range from white to brown to black, with many pattern combinations. The adult is illustrated.

Band-tailed Pigeon, *Patagioenas fasciata*
Family Columbidae (Pigeons and Doves)
Size: 14"
Season: Summer
Habitat: Mountainous pine woodlands, urban areas (sometimes)

The band-tailed pigeon is the largest pigeon found in North America, and has a heavy body with a relatively long tail and a small, rounded head. Plumage is medium brownish-gray overall, with darker wings and a purplish-brown cast to the breast. Its bill is yellow with a black tip; its eye is dark with a red orbital ring, and its nape is iridescent green, bordered above by a thin, white band. The outer half of the tail has a broad, pale band. Band-tailed pigeons consume a varied diet of insects, seeds, and berries, and voice a low, owl-like, two-part *hoo-hoooo*. The adult is illustrated.

Great Horned Owl, *Bubo virginianus*
Family Strigidae (Typical Owls)
Size: 22"
Season: Year-round
Habitat: Almost any environment, including forests, plains, and urban areas

Found throughout North America, the great horned owl is large and strong, with an obvious facial disk and sharp, long talons. Plumage is variable: Eastern forms are brown overall with heavy barring, a rust-colored face, and a white chin patch, while western forms are grayer. The prominent ear tufts give the owl its name, and its eyes are large and yellow. The great horned owl has exceptional hearing and sight. It feeds at night, perching on branches or posts and then swooping down on silent wings to catch birds, snakes, or mammals up to the size of a house cat. Its voice is a low *hoo-hoo-hoo*. The adult is illustrated.

Burrowing Owl, *Athene cunicularia*
Family Strigidae (Typical Owls)
Size: 9.5"
Season: Summer
Habitat: Open grasslands and plains

The burrowing owl is ground-dwelling, living in burrows that have been vacated by rodents or tortoises. It is small and flat-headed, and has a short tail and long legs. Plumage is brown spotted with white above, and extensively barred brown-and-white below. The owl has a white chin and throat, and bright yellow eyes. Burrowing owls can be seen day or night, perched on the ground or on posts, scanning for insects and small rodents. Sometimes they exhibit a bowing movement when approached. The voice is a chattering or cooing, and sometimes imitative of a rattlesnake. The adult is illustrated.

Belted Kingfisher, *Megaceryle alcyon*
Family Alcedinidae (Kingfishers)
Size: 13"
Season: Year-round
Habitat: Creeks, lakes

The widespread but solitary belted kingfisher is stocky and large-headed, with a long, powerful bill and a shaggy crest. It is grayish blue-green above and white below, with a thick blue band across its breast and white dotting on its back. White spots are at the lores. The female has an extra breast band of rufous hue, and is rufous along the flanks. Belted kingfishers feed by springing from a perch along the water's edge or by hovering above the water, then plunging headfirst to snatch fish, frogs, or tadpoles. Flight is uneven, and the kingfisher's vocalization is a raspy, rattling sound. The adult female is illustrated.

Lewis's Woodpecker, *Melanerpes lewis*
Family Picidae (Woodpeckers)
Size: 11"
Season: Year-round
Habitat: Open woodlands, streamsides

The Lewis's woodpecker is large and mostly dark. Plumage is greenish-black above and gray below, fading to a dusky rose on the belly. The gray of the breast continues around the neck to form a light collar. The head is dark, deep red in front surrounded by greenish-black plumage. The long, stiff tail feathers support the bird while it is perched on vertical trunks. In flight, Lewis's woodpeckers are steady and direct, not undulating like most woodpeckers. From a perch on the tree trunk, these woodpeckers fly out to catch insects, or eat nuts that they have stored in cavities. They are often seen in groups. The adult is illustrated.

Downy Woodpecker, *Picoides pubescens*
Family Picidae (Woodpeckers)
Size: 6.5"
Season: Year-round
Habitat: Woodlands, parks, urban areas, streamsides

The downy woodpecker is tiny, with a small bill and a relatively large head. It is white underneath with no barring, has black wings barred with white, and a patch of white on its back. Its head is boldly patterned in white and black, and the male sports a red nape patch. The base of the bill joins the head with fluffy nasal tufts. Juveniles may show some red on the forehead and crown. The downy woodpecker forages for berries and insects in the bark and among the smaller twigs of trees. The very similar hairy woodpecker is larger, with a longer bill and more aggressive foraging behavior, sticking to larger branches and not clinging to twigs. The adult male is illustrated.

Northern Flicker, *Colaptes auratus*
Family Picidae (Woodpeckers)
Size: 12.5"
Season: Year-round
Habitat: Variety of habitats including suburbs and parks

The common northern flicker is a large, long-tailed woodpecker often seen foraging on the ground for ants and other small insects. It is barred brown-and-black across the back, and is buff with black spotting below. Its head is brown, with a gray nape and crown. On the upper breast is a prominent half-circle of black, and the male has a red patch at the malar region. Flight is undulating and shows an orange wing lining and white rump. The flicker's voice is a loud, sharp *keee*, and it will sometimes drum its bill repeatedly at objects, like a jackhammer. It is sometimes referred to as the red-shafted flicker. The adult male is illustrated.

BIRDS: PASSERINES

Say's Phoebe, *Sayornis saya*
Family Tyrannidae (Tyrant Flycatchers)
Size: 7.5"
Season: Summer
Habitat: Arid open country, shrub land

The Say's phoebe is a fairly slim flycatcher with a long, black tail. It is pale gray-brown above, with lighter wing bars. The underside is whitish to gray under the chin and breast, fading to orange-brown on the belly and undertail coverts. Its head has a flat crown that often peaks toward the rear, and the bird has dark eyes, lores, and bill. It fly-catches for insects from a perch on rocks or twigs. The Say's phoebe voices a high, whistled *pit-eur*, and often pumps or flares out its tail. The adult is illustrated.

Western Kingbird, *Tyrannus verticalis*
Family Tyrannidae (Tyrant Flycatchers)
Size: 8.75"
Season: Summer
Habitat: Open fields, agricultural areas

The western kingbird is a relatively slender flycatcher, with a stout, black bill and a slightly rounded, black tail with white along the outer edge. It is grayish or greenish-brown above, pale gray on the breast, and bright yellow on the belly, sides, and undertail coverts. The head is light gray, with a white throat and malar area, and dark gray at the lores and behind the eye. It has a small, reddish crown patch that is normally concealed. Western kingbirds fly-catch for insects from perches on branches, posts, or wires, and the voice is composed of quick, high-pitched *zips* and *chits*. The adult is illustrated.

Blue Jay, *Cyanocitta cristata*
Family Corvidae (Jays and Crows)
Size: 11"
Season: Year-round in northeastern Colorado
Habitat: Woodlands, rural and urban areas

The solitary blue jay is sturdy and crested. It is bright blue above and white below, with a thick, tapered, black bill. There is a white patch around the eye that extends to the chin, bordered by a thin, black "necklace" extending to the nape. The blue jay has a conspicuous white wing bar, and dark barring on the wings and tail. In flight the white outer edges of the tail are visible. The jay alternates shallow wing beats with glides. Omnivorous, the blue jay eats just about anything, but especially consumes acorns, nuts, fruits, insects, and small vertebrates. It is a raucous and noisy bird, and quite bold. Sometimes it mimics the calls of birds of prey. The adult is illustrated.

Steller's Jay, *Cyanocitta stelleri*
Family Corvidae (Jays and Crows)
Size: 11.5"
Season: Year-round
Habitat: Coniferous forests, mountainous areas

The Steller's jay is bold, stocky, and crested, with short, broad wings. The tail, back, wings, and belly are bright, deep blue, while the mantle and breast are sooty gray. The black head has a thick, pointed crest, and inland races have white eyebrows and thin white streaks on the forehead. The legs and bill are stout and strong. Steller's jays eat a wide variety of food, from nuts, insects, and berries to picnic scraps. The voice is a loud, raucous squawking, and they sometimes mimic the calls of other birds. The adult is illustrated.

Western Scrub Jay, *Aphelocoma californica*
Family Corvidae (Jays and Crows)
Size: 11.5"
Season: Year-round
Habitat: Open areas of scrub oak, urban areas

The western scrub jay is long-necked, sleek, and crestless. Its upperparts are deep blue, with a distinct, lighter gray-brown mantle. Its underparts are pale gray, becoming white on the belly and undertail coverts. It has a thin, white superciliary stripe, the malar area is dark gray, and the throat is streaked with white-and-gray above a dull gray "necklace" across the breast. The bird's flight is an undulating combination of rapid wing beats and swooping glides. Its diet consists of nuts, seeds, insects, and fruit. The adult is illustrated.

Clark's Nutcracker, *Nucifraga columbiana*
Family Corvidae (Jays and Crows)
Size: 12"
Season: Year-round
Habitat: Coniferous forests of high mountain areas

The Clark's nutcracker is a chunky, wily, crestless jay with long wings and a stout, thick-based bill. Plumage is gray or brownish-gray overall, with black wings and a two-toned, black-and-white tail. There is a prominent white patch on the outer secondary feathers. The head has deep black eyes surrounded by whitish areas, and a black bill. Clark's nutcrackers forage in trees and along the ground for pine nuts, insects, and fruit, but will also scavenge at picnic grounds. They walk with a swaying, crowlike gait, and voice loud, harsh, rattling squawks. The adult is illustrated.

Black-billed Magpie, *Pica hudsonia*
Family Corvidae (Jays and Crows)
Size: 19"
Season: Year-round
Habitat: Riparian areas, open woodlands, pastures, rural areas

The black-billed magpie is heavy and broad-winged, with an extremely long, graduated tail. It has striking pied plumage, being black on the head, upper breast, and back, dark, iridescent green-blue on the wings and tail, and crisp white on the scapulars and belly. Its legs are dark and stout, and the bill is thick at the base. Juvenile birds have a much shorter tail. Magpies travel in small groups and are opportunistic feeders, eating insects, nuts, eggs, or carrion. The voice is a whining, questioning *mag?* or a harsh *wok-wok*. The adult is illustrated.

American Crow, *Corvus brachyrhynchos*
Family Corvidae (Jays and Crows)
Size: 17.5"
Season: Year-round
Habitat: Open woodlands, pastures, rural fields, dumps

The American crow is widespread, found across the continent. Known for its familiar, loud, grating *caw, caw* vocalization, the crow is a large, stocky bird with a short, rounded tail, broad wings, and a thick, powerful bill. Plumage is glistening black overall, in all stages of development. It will eat almost anything, and often forms loose flocks with other crows. The adult is illustrated.

Horned Lark, *Eremophila alpestris*
Family Alaudidae (Larks)
Size: 7"
Season: Year-round
Habitat: Open and barren country

The horned lark is slim and elongated, with long wings. Its plumage is pale reddish-gray above and whitish below, with variable amounts of rusty smudging or streaking on the breast and sides. The head is boldly patterned with a black crown, cheek patch, and breast bar, contrasting with a yellow throat and white face. In females the black markings are much paler. Particularly evident on males, there are feather tufts, or "horns," on the sides of the crown. Outer tail feathers are black. Horned larks are ground-dwelling birds, scurrying on the ground while foraging for plant matter and insects. They sing with rapid, musical warbles and chips. The adult male is illustrated.

Tree Swallow, *Tachycineta bicolor*
Family Hirundinidae (Swallows)
Size: 5.75"
Season: Summer
Habitat: Variety of habitats near water and perching sites

The tree swallow has a short, slightly notched tail, broad-based triangular wings, and a thick neck. It has a high-contrast plumage pattern, with dark, metallic green-blue upperparts and crisp white underparts. When perched, the primaries reach just past the tail tip. Juveniles are gray-brown below, with a subtle, darker breast band. Tree swallows take insects on the wing, but will also eat berries and fruits. The voice is a high-pitched chirping. The swallows often are seen in huge lines of individuals perched on wires or branches. The adult male is illustrated.

Barn Swallow, *Hirundo rustica*
Family Hirundinidae (Swallows)
Size: 6.5"
Season: Summer
Habitat: Old buildings, caves, open rural areas near bridges

Widespread and common, the barn swallow has narrow, pointed wings and a long, deeply forked tail. It is pale below and dark blue above, with a rusty orange forehead and throat. In males the underparts are pale orange, while females are a pale cream color below. Barn swallows are graceful, fluid fliers, and they often forage in groups to catch insects in flight. The voice is a loud, repetitive chirping or clicking. They build cup-shaped nests of mud on almost any protected man-made structure. The adult male is illustrated.

Black-capped Chickadee, *Poecile atricapillus*
Family Paridae (Chickadees and Titmice)
Size: 5.25"
Season: Year-round
Habitat: Mixed woodlands, rural gardens, feeders

The black-capped chickadee is small, compact, and active, with short, rounded wings and a tiny black bill. It is gray above and lighter gray or dusky below, with a contrasting black cap and throat patch. It is quite similar to the eastern Carolina chickadee, which does not normally occur in Colorado. Its voice sounds like its name—*chick-a-dee-dee-dee*—or is a soft *fee-bay*. The chickadee is quite social, and feeds on a variety of seeds, berries, and insects found in trees and shrubs. The adult is illustrated.

Mountain Chickadee, *Poecile gambeli*
Family Paridae (Chickadees and Titmice)
Size: 5.25"
Season: Year-round
Habitat: Mountainous woodlands

The mountain chickadee is small and fluffy with a tiny bill. It is similar to the black-capped chickadee, but with a white superciliary stripe through its black cap. It is grayish above, with pale gray or buff-colored underparts, and has a black crown and chin patch. Energetic and acrobatic, the mountain chickadee travels in small groups eating small insects and seeds gleaned from tree branches. Its voice sounds like *chick-a-dee-dee-dee*. The adult is illustrated.

White-breasted Nuthatch, *Sitta carolinensis*
Family Sittidae (Nuthatches)
Size: 5.75"
Season: Year-round
Habitat: Mixed oak or coniferous woodlands

The white-breasted nuthatch has a large head and a wide neck, short, rounded wings, and a short tail. It is blue-gray above and pale gray below, with rusty smudging on the lower flanks and undertail coverts. The breast and face are white, and a black crown merges with the mantle. The bill is long, thin, and upturned at the tip. To forage, the white-breasted nuthatch creeps head first down tree trunks to pick out insects and seeds. Its voice is a nasal, repetitive *auk, auk, auk*. It nests in tree cavities high off the ground. The adult male is illustrated.

Brown Creeper, *Certhia americana*
Family Certhiidae (Creepers)
Size: 5.25"
Season: Year-round
Habitat: Mature woodlands

The brown creeper is a small, cryptically colored bird with a long, pointed tail and a long, down-curved bill. It is mottled black, brown, and white above, and is plain white below, fading to brownish toward the rear. Its face has a pale supercilium and a white chin. The legs are short, with long, grasping toes. Brown creepers spiral upward on tree trunks, probing for insects in the bark, then fly to the bottom of another tree to repeat the process. Its stiff tail aids in propping the bird up, like a woodpecker's tail. The creeper's voice is composed of thin, high-pitched *seet* notes. The adult is illustrated.

Marsh Wren, *Cistothorus palustris*
Family Troglodytidae (Wrens)
Size: 5"
Season: Year-round
Habitat: Marshes, reeds, stream banks

The marsh wren is small and cryptic, with a normally cocked-up tail. The color is rufous brown; the tail and wings are barred with black, and the chin and breast are white. A well-defined white superciliary stripe runs below a uniform brown crown, and the mantle shows distinct black-and-white striping. The bill is long and slightly decurved. Marsh wrens are vocal day and night, voicing quick, repetitive cheeping. They are secretive but inquisitive, and glean insects from the marsh vegetation and the water surface. The adult is illustrated.

Rock Wren, *Salpinctes obsoletus*
Family Troglodytidae (Wrens)
Size: 6"
Season: Summer; year-round in southwestern Colorado
Habitat: Deserts; open, dry, rocky areas

The rock wren is stocky, with a short tail, a large head, and a thin, slightly down-curved bill. It is grayish brown above, with fine barring and spotting. Its underparts are pale buff to gray, with fine streaking along the breast and dark bars on the undertail coverts. There is a pale superciliary stripe above the dark eye. The pale brownish tips of the outer tail feathers are visible when the tail is fanned. Rock wrens search around rocks for insects, flitting from rock to rock and often bobbing up and down. The adult is illustrated.

American Dipper, *Cinclus mexicanus*
Family Cinclidae (Dippers)
Size: 7.5"
Season: Year-round
Habitat: Near fast-flowing, rocky, mountainous streams

The American dipper is an unusual, plump, aquatic songbird with a short tail, long legs, and a short, thin bill. The plumage is dense and usually disheveled, slate-gray overall, with a brownish hue on the head. Thin, white crescents are sometimes visible around the dark eyes. Dippers perch on rocks in a stream and plunge into the water, propelled by their wings, to pick out larvae and insects. Sometimes they use their long toes to cling to underwater rocks. They fly low above the water surface, and course up and down stream corridors. While perched, they constantly bob their bodies up and down. The dipper is also known as the water ouzel. The adult is illustrated.

Golden-crowned Kinglet, *Regulus satrapa*
Family Regulidae (Kinglets)
Size: 4"
Season: Year-round
Habitat: Mixed woodlands, brushy areas

The golden-crowned kinglet is a tiny, plump songbird with a short tail and a short, pointed bill. It is greenish-gray above, with wings patterned in black, white, and green, and pale gray below. The face has a dark eye stripe and crown, and the center of the crown is golden yellow and sometimes raised. The legs are dark, with orange toes. Kinglets are in constant motion, flitting and dangling among branches, sometimes hanging upside down or hovering at the edges of branches to feed. The voice includes very high-pitched *tzee* notes. The adult is illustrated.

Townsend's Solitaire, *Myadestes townsendi*
Family Turdidae (Thrushes)
Size: 8.5"
Season: Year-round
Habitat: Mountainous coniferous woodlands, juniper scrub

The Townsend's solitaire is a slim, elongated thrush with a short, blunt bill. It often perches upright on bare branches with its long tail drooping down. It is grayish overall, darker on the wings and tail, with buff-colored patches at the base of its flight feathers. Its eyes are dark, with distinctive white eye rings. White outer tail feathers are evident on the fanned tail. The juvenile is darker, with extensive light spotting. Townsend's solitaires forage for insects, seeds, and pine nuts. The adult is illustrated.

Mountain Bluebird, *Sialia currucoides*
Family Turdidae (Thrushes)
Size: 7.25"
Season: Year-round
Habitat: Open mountain meadows, sage land

Compared to other bluebirds, the mountain bluebird has a thinner bill, a longer tail, and longer wings. The male is bright, sky-blue overall, somewhat paler below, and nearly white at the undertail coverts. The female retains the blue color on the tail and wings, but is pale gray on her back, underparts, and head, with a noticeable white eye ring. Juveniles are similar to females, but darker on the back and spotted below. From perches on branches or posts, mountain bluebirds dart out to catch insects. They form large winter flocks and tend to hold their bodies in a horizontal posture. The adult male is illustrated.

American Robin, *Turdus migratorius*
Family Turdidae (Thrushes)
Size: 10"
Season: Year-round
Habitat: Widespread in a variety of habitats, including woodlands, fields, parks, lawns

Familiar and friendly, the American robin is a large thrush with long legs and a long tail. It commonly holds its head cocked and keeps its wing tips lowered beneath its tail. It is gray-brown above and rufous below, with a darker head and contrasting white eye crescents and loral patches. The chin is streaked black and white, and the bill is yellow with darker edges. Females are typically paler overall, and the juvenile shows spots of white above and dark spots below. Robins forage on the ground for earthworms and insects, and in trees for berries. The robin's song is a series of high, musical phrases, sounding like *cheery, cheer-u-up, cheerio.* The adult male is illustrated.

Hermit Thrush, *Catharus guttatus*
Family Turdidae (Thrushes)
Size: 7"
Season: Summer
Habitat: Woodlands, brushy areas

The hermit thrush is compact and habitually cocks its short tail. It forages on the ground near vegetative cover for insects, worms, and berries, and voices a song of beautiful, flutelike notes. It is reddish to olive-brown above, with a rufous tail. Its underparts are white, with dusky flanks and sides and black spotting on its throat and breast. Its dark eyes are encircled by white eye rings. In flight the pale wing lining contrasts with the dark flight feathers. Adult is illustrated.

Yellow-rumped Warbler, *Dendroica coronata*
Family Parulidae (Wood Warblers)
Size: 5.5"
Season: Summer
Habitat: Deciduous and coniferous woodlands, suburbs with wax myrtle

Two races of this species occur in North America. The "myrtle" form is dispersed across North America, and the "Audubon's" form is seen west of the Rockies. The myrtle variety is blue-gray above, with dark streaks, and white below, with black streaking below the chin and a bright yellow side patch. There is a black mask across the face, bordered by a thin superciliary stripe above and a white throat below. The nonbreeding adult male and female are paler, with a more brownish cast to the upperparts. The longish tail has white spots on either side and meets with the conspicuous yellow rump. The Audubon's variety has a yellow chin and a gray face. Yellow-rumped warblers prefer to eat berries and insects. The adult male myrtle form is illustrated.

Common Yellowthroat, *Geothlypis trichas*
Family Parulidae (Wood Warblers)
Size: 5"
Season: Summer
Habitat: Swamps, fields, low vegetation near water

The common yellowthroat scampers through the undergrowth looking for insects and spiders in a somewhat wrenlike manner. It is a plump little warbler that often cocks up its tail. Plumage is olive-brown above, pale brown to whitish below, with a bright yellow breast/chin region and undertail coverts. The male has a black facial mask trailed by a fuzzy white area on the nape. Females lack the facial mask. The male, below, and female, above, are illustrated.

Yellow-breasted Chat, *Icteria virens*
Family Parulidae (Wood Warblers)
Size: 7.5"
Season: Summer
Habitat: Dense vegetation, woodland edges

The largest wood warbler, the yellow-breasted chat has a long, rounded tail and a heavy, black, pointed bill with a strongly curved culmen. It is uniformly greenish-brown above, its belly and undertail coverts are white, and its chin and breast are bright yellow. The head is dark, with bold white patterning above the lores, at the malar area, and around the eye, forming white "spectacles." Females are slightly duller in color. Yellow-breasted chats forage in low brush for insects and berries, and have quite variable vocalizations, including mimicking the songs of other birds. The male has a strange display behavior in which he hovers and dangles his legs. The adult is illustrated.

Spotted Towhee, *Pipilo maculatus*
Family Emberizidae (Sparrows and Buntings)
Size: 8.5"
Season: Year-round
Habitat: Thickets, suburban shrubs, gardens

The spotted towhee is a large, long-tailed sparrow with a thick, short bill and sturdy legs. It forages on the ground in dense cover by kicking back both feet at once to uncover insects, seeds, and worms. It is black above, including the head and upper breast, and has rufous sides and a white belly. It has white wing bars, white spotting on its scapulars and mantle, and white corners on its tail. The eye color is red. Females are like the males, but are brown above. The spotted towhee was once conspecific with the eastern towhee, known as the rufous-sided towhee. The adult male is illustrated.

Lark Sparrow, *Chondestes grammacus*
Family Emberizidae (Sparrows and Buntings)
Size: 6.5"
Season: Summer
Habitat: Woodland edges, dry prairies with brush, agricultural areas

The lark sparrow is elongate and thin, with a long, rounded tail. It is brown above, streaked with dark brown, and white below, with tan around its sides and flanks. There is a distinct dark spot in the middle of its breast. Its head is patterned with a rufous crown that has a white medial stripe; it has rufous cheeks, black eye lines, and a black throat stripe. Lark sparrows travel in small flocks, hopping or walking on the ground to pick up seeds and insects. They sing a variety of high-pitched chips and trills, often from a conspicuous perch. Males may display with their tails cocked up. The adult is illustrated.

Song Sparrow, *Melospiza melodia*
Family Emberizidae (Sparrows and Buntings)
Size: 6"
Season: Year-round
Habitat: Thickets, shrubs, woodland edges near water

One of the most common sparrows, the song sparrow is fairly plump, with a long, rounded tail. It is brown and gray with streaking above, and white below, with heavy dark or brownish streaking that often congeals into a discrete spot in the middle of its breast. Its head has a dark crown with a gray medial stripe, dark eye lines, and a dark malar stripe above the white chin. Song sparrows are usually seen in small groups or individually, foraging on the ground for insects and seeds. The song is a series of chips and trills of variable pitch, and the call is a *chip, chip, chip*. The adult is illustrated.

Dark-eyed Junco, *Junco hyemalis*
Family Emberizidae (Sparrows and Buntings)
Size: 6.5"
Season: Winter
Habitat: Thickets, rural gardens, open coniferous or mixed woodlands

The dark-eyed junco is a small, plump sparrow with a short, conical, pink bill and several distinct variations in plumage. One of the more common races is the "Oregon" junco, with its rusty brown mantle, sides, and flanks, white belly, and black head and breast. Sexes are similar, but the female is paler overall. The white outer tail feathers are obvious in flight. Juncos hop about on the ground, often in groups, picking up insects and seeds. The voice is a staccato, monotone, chirping trill. Also common in Colorado is the gray-headed junco, which is pale gray overall, with a rufous mantle. The adult male of the Oregon race is illustrated.

Western Tanager, *Piranga ludoviciana*
Family Cardinalidae (Tanagers, Cardinals, and Grosbeaks)
Size: 7.25"
Season: Summer
Habitat: Mixed or coniferous woodlands

The western tanager is a highly arboreal, brightly colored tanager with pointed wings and a short but thick bill. The breeding male has a black upper back, tail, and wings, with a yellow shoulder patch and a white wing bar. His underside and rump are bright yellow, extending across the neck and nape, and his head is red-orange. Females and winter males are paler, with little or no red on the head. Western tanagers forage for insects, primarily in the upper canopies of mature trees. They are usually difficult to see clearly, but their vocalizations—three-syllabled, rattling high notes with changing accents—are distinctive. The breeding adult male is illustrated.

Western Meadowlark, *Sturnella neglecta*
Family Icteridae (Blackbirds, Orioles, and Grackles)
Size: 9.5"
Season: Year-round
Habitat: Open fields, grasslands, meadows

The western meadowlark is chunky and short-tailed, with a flat head and a long, pointed bill. It is heavily streaked and barred above, and yellow beneath with dark streaking. The head has a dark crown, white superciliary stripes, dark eye lines, and a yellow chin and malar area. A black, V-shaped "necklace" that becomes quite pale during winter months is on the upper breast. Non-breeding plumage is much paler overall. Meadowlarks gather in loose flocks to pick through grasses for insects and seeds. They often perch on telephone wires or posts and sing short, whistling phrases. The breeding adult is illustrated.

Red-winged Blackbird, *Agelaius phoeniceus*
Family Icteridae (Blackbirds, Orioles, and Grackles)
Size: 8.5"
Season: Year-round
Habitat: Marshes, meadows, agricultural areas near water

The red-winged blackbird is a widespread, ubiquitous, chunky meadow dweller that forms huge flocks during the nonbreeding season. The male is deep black overall, with bright orange-red lesser coverts and pale medial coverts that form an obvious shoulder patch in flight, but may be partially concealed on the perched bird. The female is barred in tan and dark brown overall, with pale superciliary stripes and a pale malar patch. The blackbirds forage marshlands for insects, spiders, and seeds. The voice is a loud, raspy, vibrating *konk-a-leee* given from a perch atop a tall reed or branch. The male, below, and female, above, are illustrated.

123

Brewer's Blackbird, *Euphagus cyanocephalus*
Family Icteridae (Blackbirds, Orioles, and Grackles)
Size: 9"
Season: Year-round
Habitat: Meadows, pastures, open woodlands, urban areas

The Brewer's blackbird is small-headed and dark, with a short bill and bright yellow eyes (in males). The breeding male is glossy black overall, with purple iridescence on the head and breast, and green iridescence on the wings and tail. During winter the plumage is not as glossy. Females are drab brownish overall, and usually have dark eyes. Brewer's blackbirds forage on the ground for seeds and insects, often while bowed over with their tails sticking up. The voice is a short, coarse *zhet,* and a longer, creaky trill. These blackbirds form large flocks in winter, along with other blackbird species. The breeding adult male is illustrated.

Evening Grosbeak, *Coccothraustes vespertinus*
Family Fringillidae (Finches)
Size: 8"
Season: Year-round
Habitat: Coniferous or mixed woodlands, rural gardens

The evening grosbeak is a comical-looking finch, with a large head, a short stubby tail, and an enormous conical bill. In the male, plumage fades from dark brown on the head to bright yellow toward the rump and belly. His wings are black, with large white patches on the secondaries and tertials. The yellow superciliums merge with his flat forehead and meet his pale, yellow-green bill. The legs are short and pinkish. Females are grayish overall, with choppy white markings on the wings. Evening grosbeaks travel in flocks to feed on seeds and berries in the upper canopy, and will often visit feeders, preferring sunflower seeds. The voice is a series of short, spaced, rattling *cheep* notes. The male, below, and female, above, are illustrated.

Pine Siskin, *Carduelis pinus*
Family Fringillidae (Finches)
Size: 5"
Season: Year-round
Habitat: Coniferous woodlands, rural gardens

The pine siskin is a small, cryptically colored finch with a short tail and a narrow, pointed bill. The male's head and back are light brown overall, heavily streaked with darker brown. His underside is whitish and streaked in darker shades. There is a prominent yellow wing bar on the greater coverts, and yellow on the flight feather edges and at the base of the primaries. Females are marked similarly, with a darker underside and white—not yellow—wing bars. Individuals can be quite variable as to the amount of streaking and the prominence of the yellow coloring. Pine siskins forage energetically in small groups for seeds and insects, sometimes clinging upside down on twigs to reach food. The voice consists of high-pitched, erratic, raspy chips and trills. The adult male is illustrated.

REPTILES

Side-blotched Lizard, *Uta stansburiana*
Family Phrynosomatidae (Horned Lizards and Allies)
Size: Up to 6"
Range: Western Colorado
Habitat: Dry, rocky, or sandy areas; grasslands; chaparral

The side-blotched lizard is common in the arid western regions. It is small, with a long, tapered tail, long toes on its hind legs, external ear openings, and a distinct fold of skin on its throat (the gular fold). The color is generally brownish or gray, which can be uniform or interrupted with a variety of spots, stripes, or chevrons. Dark blue or black blotches are on the sides of the body, just behind the front legs, for which the lizard gets its name. Males also have gray and orange stripes on their throats and blue-gray speckling across their backs and tails. These lizards are active during the day, basking on rocks or logs and hopping or running among rocks, preying on small invertebrates including insects and scorpions. The male is illustrated.

Texas Horned Lizard, *Phrynosoma cornutum*
Family Phrynosomatidae (Horned Lizards and Allies)
Size: Up to 7", including tail
Range: Southern and eastern Colorado
Habitat: Arid habitats with sparse vegetation

The Texas horned lizard is one of more than a dozen species of horned lizards (sometimes erroneously called "horned toads") adapted to harsh, arid conditions and adorned with fearsome, pointed scales and horns. The lizard's body is flattened; it has a short, tapered tail, long central "crown" horns at the top of its head, two rows of fringed scales along its sides, and is coarse and spiny overall. The color is any variation of earth tones, with darker splotches behind the neck, on the back, and on the tail. A pale stripe runs down the center of the back, and dark lines radiate from the eyes. Texas horned lizards are active during the day, preying mostly on ants, termites, and other small insects. They find shelter by burrowing in loose soil or hiding beneath bushes and rocks.

Eastern Fence Lizard, *Sceloporus undulatus*
Family Phrynosomatidae (Horned Lizards and Allies)
Size: Up to 6"
Range: Throughout Colorado
Habitat: A wide variety of sunny habitats, including grasslands, woodlands, brushy areas

The eastern fence lizard includes several subspecies of varying color patterns, including grayish or brownish, with longitudinal striping, spotting, or a combination of the two. In Colorado, these common lizards are sometimes called blue-bellies because the males show blue patches on the belly and chin. The fence lizard is compact and long-tailed, with big feet, a blunt face, and scaled, dry skin. Solitary and active during the day, fence lizards scurry through sheltered areas or among trees, feeding on all kinds of insects and other invertebrates.

Collared Lizard, *Crotaphytus collaris*
Family Crotaphytidae (Collared and Leopard Lizards)
Size: Up to 14"
Range: Southwestern and southeastern Colorado
Habitat: Dry, rocky areas

Also known as the "mountain boomer," the collared lizard is chunky and colorful, with a large head, large limbs, a long, narrow, rounded tail, and smooth, granular scales. Its most distinctive mark is a black-and-white collar band on the back of its neck. Otherwise color and patterning are quite variable, but usually the lizard is yellowish, tan, or blue green, with small spots on the body, tail, legs, and face, and light banding across the back. Breeding females show orange markings along their sides. Collared lizards leap from rock to rock or run on open ground on their hind legs with their tails raised, looking like quick little dinosaurs. To feed, the collared lizard ambushes smaller lizards and insects, which it subdues with powerful jaws.

Long-nosed Leopard Lizard, *Gambelia wislizenii*
Family Crotaphytidae (Collared and Leopard Lizards)
Size: Up to 15"
Range: Southwestern Colorado
Habitat: Arid, sandy, or gravelly areas with sparse vegetation

This leopard lizard is fairly large, agile, and stout, with a large head and limbs and a long, rounded tail. The snout is long and the scales are smooth and granular. The color is brown to gray above, paler below, with variable markings depending on the region. In general, the lizard has light crossbars along its back and an overall speckling of dark brown "leopard spots" on its tail, head, and body. In cool temperatures the skin may become noticeably darker; during breeding, males develop reddish bellies, while females have reddish markings on their sides. Active during the day, leopard lizards scamper quickly along the ground and bush, preying on insects and other lizards.

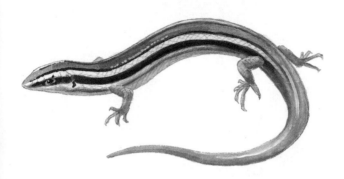

Western Skink, *Eumeces skiltonianus*
Family Scincidae (Skinks)
Size: Up to 9", including tail
Range: West of the Rocky Mountains
Habitat: A wide variety of habitats, including woodlands, streamsides, fields

Like the other skinks, the western skink has a long, narrow, cylindrical body, a long, tapering tail, small limbs, and smooth, shiny scales. It is distinctively colored with a broad, brown stripe down its back, blackish stripes along its sides, and pale stripes between these. The tail is bright blue in juveniles, becoming grayish in mature individuals. Breeding males develop orange markings under the chin and on the belly. Active during the day, western skinks usually stay hidden under leaves, rocks, or stumps. They feed on insects, spiders, sowbugs, earthworms, and other invertebrates. They also dig burrows and remain in them for winter in cold climates.

Six-lined Racerunner, *Cnemidophorus sexlineatus*
Family Teiidae (Whiptails and Racerunners)
Size: Up to 10", including tail
Range: Lower latitudes east of the Rocky Mountains
Habitat: Fields with sparse vegetation, open woodlands, rocky areas, streamsides

Closely related to the western whiptail, the six-lined racerunner has the same long, narrow body, long limbs, and very long, thin, whiplike tail. The body is lined with alternating yellowish or whitish stripes and brown to black stripes, often with a brown stripe along the middle of the back. The underparts are white in females, while males show a blue-green wash on the belly, foreparts, and throat. The tail is blue in juveniles and brownish in adults. Active in the daytime, six-lined racerunners bask in the sun and feed on insects and other invertebrates. They are very quick and agile, using speed to avoid capture. They seek the shelter of burrows when temperatures are colder.

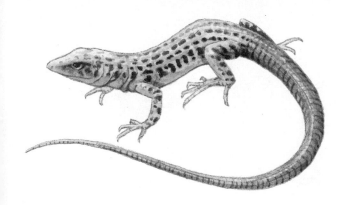

Western Whiptail, *Cnemidophorus tigris*
Family Teiidae (Whiptails and Racerunners)
Size: Up to 12"
Range: Western Colorado
Habitat: Arid, open areas, open woodlands

Whiptails are known for their quick and jerky movements, relatively long, slender bodies, large limbs, and long, thin, whiplike
tails. Several subspecies with variations in color and pattern exist,
but all generally show dark spotting or marbling on the head and
body over a grayish, yellowish, or brownish background, with several paler, longitudinal stripes down the back and sides. The belly
and throat are normally whitish to pale yellow but in some cases
may be nearly black. The tail is blue in juveniles, fading to pale
gray in adults. Active during the day, western whiptails feed on
insects and spiders in leaf litter or underground. Wary by nature,
they run rapidly to avoid danger, often seeking the protection of
brush or burrows, and will detach their tails if attacked.

Rubber Boa, *Charina bottae*
Family Boidae (Boas)
Size: Up to 30"
Range: Northwestern Colorado
Habitat: A wide variety of habitats including woodlands, meadows, and streamsides

In addition to the rosy boa, the rubber boa is the only other member of this family native to the United States, preferring the cool, moist conditions it finds here. It has a stout, muscular body, tiny eyes with vertical pupils, a small, blunt head, and a thick, blunt tail tip that resembles another head. The scales are small, sleek, and smooth, giving the appearance of rubber. The color is unmarked brown, reddish, or greenish-gray above, and yellow along the underside. Secretive and docile, the rubber boa will burrow or hide under leaves, rocks, or rotten wood if threatened. It will curl into a ball with its head buried and tail exposed when provoked, almost never biting as a defense. Active during night or twilight, the boa moves on the ground or in trees, or it swims. It uses constriction to subdue its prey of shrews, other small mammals, and birds; it also eats eggs.

Northern Water Snake, *Nerodia sipedon*
Family Colubridae (Colubrid Snakes)
Size: Up to 50"
Range: Eastern Colorado
Habitat: Most freshwater habitats including streams, lakes, swamps

The northern water snake is aquatic, thick-bodied, and quite common in its range. Its color is highly variable, but is usually light to dark brown or gray, with broad, darker, brown, black or reddish bands behind its neck, and broken bands or mottling along the rest of its body. Its underside is paler, often with crescent-shaped markings. Older snakes become nearly black overall. Active at all times of the day or night, the snakes are seen basking on rocks and logs near water, or pursuing all manner of aquatic prey including frogs, minnows, salamanders, and crayfish. Although not poisonous, bites can be painful and, because of an anticoagulant released in the bite, wounds may bleed profusely.

Racer, *Coluber constrictor*
Family Colubridae (Colubrid Snakes)
Size: Up to 60"
Range: Eastern Colorado
Habitat: Brush and thickets, often near water, and in suburbs

With nearly a dozen subspecies, each with a different coloration, the racer is often sighted in residential areas. It is a long, thin, speedy snake; its eyes are dark and relatively large, the neck is thin, and the scales are smooth. Its color can be black, dark gray, bluish-green, or brownish above, paler below, often with a whitish throat area. Young snakes are paler overall, with rounded, brownish spots along the back. Burrowing during the night, racers are most active in the daytime, foraging on the ground for insects or small vertebrates. They are capable of climbing trees to escape danger. Although not poisonous, they are capable of inflicting painful bites.

Milk Snake, *Lampropeltis triangulum*
Family Colubridae (Colubrid Snakes)
Size: Up to 60"
Range: Eastern Colorado
Habitat: Highly variable depending on region; forests, fields, wetlands, streamsides, farmland

One of the most widespread snakes in the United States, the milk snake is narrow-bodied, with a small head and smooth scales. There is much geographical variation in color and pattern, but black-bordered, reddish or brown bands or blotches appear over a yellowish, tan, or pale gray background. The lighter background color is widest toward the base. In many cases there is a V-shaped mark on the top of the head, and the belly may have a distinct, black-and-white pattern. Active day or night, favoring covered areas under logs or in rocks, milk snakes prey on small mammals, eggs, and other reptiles, subduing them by constriction and suffocation. The common name is derived from the myth that they suck the milk of cows.

Long-nosed Snake, *Rhinocheilus lecontei*
Family Colubridae (Colubrid Snakes)
Size: Up to 40"
Range: Southeastern Colorado
Habitat: Arid grasslands, scrubland, chaparral

The long-nosed snake is medium-size, thin, smooth-scaled, and can be found in the desert and semi-arid regions of the Southwest and Great Basin, as well as southeastern Colorado. The head is scarcely wider than the body, and the snout is pointed, with a countersunk lower jaw. The color varies regionally, but in general is creamy yellow, with broad, black saddles speckled with lighter color. Reddish coloring appears between these saddles, and black speckling appears on the snake's sides. Some varieties lack the reddish color, being only black and creamy white. Long-nosed snakes stay under rocks or in underground burrows during the day, venturing out at night to hunt for small reptiles, eggs, mammals, and insects. In winter months, they can be found hibernating underground. If alarmed, these snakes will assume a defensive posture in which the body coils and writhes, the tail quivers, and fluids are emitted from the anus.

Corn Snake, *Elaphe guttata*
Family Colubridae (Colubrid Snakes)
Size: Up to 72"
Range: Southeastern Colorado
Habitat: Quite variable; streamsides, woodlands, rocky slopes, farmlands

Also known as the red rat snake, the corn snake is handsome and long-bodied, with a docile disposition, and is popular in the pet trade. Eastern individuals are brownish yellow, with dark-bordered, orange or reddish saddlelike marks down the back and smaller marks along the sides. Farther west, the background color is more grayish, with brown marks. In all varieties, the underside is paler with dark speckles, and the top of the head usually sports a pointed mark between the eyes. Staying in burrows, crevices, or under rocks at night, corn snakes become active at daytime, searching for small mammals, birds, bats, and reptiles, which they subdue by constriction. The common name is derived from the fact that these snakes are found near corn storage areas, attracted to the rodents that feed there.

Striped Whipsnake, *Masticophis taeniatus*
Family Colubridae (Colubrid Snakes)
Size: Up to 72"
Range: Western Colorado
Habitat: Deserts, sage land, rocky areas, mountains, grasslands

Related to the racers, the striped whipsnake is aggressive and speedy. Its body is long and thin, like a bull whip, with a narrow, tapering tail and smooth scales. It has large, round eyes. The color is brownish, gray, or nearly black above, with two pale yellow or white stripes along each side, along with a broken (or solid), thin, dark stripe in between. The underside is whitish, pale pink, or yellowish. Active during the day, the striped whipsnake moves along the ground or in trees feeding on other reptiles, small mammals, insects, or birds. It hibernates during cold weather in burrows or under rocks. Striped whipsnakes usually speed away into the brush or rocks if provoked, and although not venomous, will readily bite.

Ringneck Snake, *Diadophis punctatus*
Family Colubridae (Colubrid Snakes)
Size: Up to 30"
Range: Southeastern Colorado
Habitat: Quite varied; found mostly in moist areas in woodlands, fields, scrub, and along streams

The ringneck snake is small, thin, and smooth, with a dozen or so subspecies found across the United States. All varieties are characterized by a uniform gray to brownish upper surface, a bright yellow-orange or red underside (brightest on the tail), a dark head, and a conspicuous yellow-orange neck ring. The neck ring may be complete or broken, and the belly is often marked with black spots. Secretive, the ringneck snake keeps to moist areas of its habitat, with a cover of rocks, leaf litter, rotting stumps, and burrows. It feeds on small prey such as insects, worms, and small vertebrates. A common defense posture includes lifting its front parts, supported by a coiled rear, to expose its bright underside.

Gopher Snake, *Pituophis catenifer*
Family Colubridae (Colubrid Snakes)
Size: 48"–96"
Range: Lower elevations of Colorado
Habitat: Desert, pine-oak woodlands, rocky areas, scrubland, prairies

The gopher snake is widespread, large, and powerful. It has more than a dozen subspecies, and goes by many common names, including pine snake, pine-gopher, and bull snake. Its body is thick, with ridged scales on the upper surface; the eyes have round pupils. The base color is light brown, pale gray, or yellowish, heavily marked with reddish-brown or blackish blotches and spots. Some varieties are nearly solid black; others have distinct, lengthwise stripes. Chiefly active during the day, gopher snakes hide in rodent or tortoise burrows, crevices, or under rocks during the day but often are found during the night in warm weather. They hunt on the ground, in trees, or in burrows for rodents and other reptiles, leaping at prey and constricting it with their strong bodies. If confronted, the gopher snake will flatten its head, hiss, and quiver its tail.

Common Garter Snake, *Thamnophis sirtalis*
Family Colubridae (Colubrid Snakes)
Size: Up to 40"
Range: Northeastern and south-central Colorado
Habitat: Well-vegetated areas near water, marshes, urban parks

The common garter snake is, true to its name, widespread and common, with more than ten subspecies that commonly frequent developed areas and home gardens. It is a thin, medium-size snake with a head slightly wider that its body and relatively large eyes. The skin has keeled scales and is extremely variable in color, depending on subspecies, but always shows three longitudinal stripes—one running across the top of the back, and two along the sides. Often there are blackish spots between the stripes. The underparts are pale. Garter snakes freely move from land to water. They feed on insects, aquatic invertebrates, fish, and small mammals. They are relatively harmless but can bite and may emit foul-smelling fluid if trapped.

Western Rattlesnake, *Crotalus viridis*
Family Viperidae (Pit Vipers)
Size: Up to 62"
Range: Throughout Colorado
Habitat: Quite variable depending on region: forests, sand dunes, grasslands, rocky areas up to timberline

The western rattlesnake is a thick, rough-scaled, venomous pit viper with a flat, wide, triangular head, retractable fangs, and a tail tipped with horny segments that buzz when shaken. This species comprises several subspecies with variable colorations and sizes. The background color can be pale yellow, brown, reddish, greenish, or dark gray, with darker, light-edged blotches along the back that merge to cross bands on the tail. There is usually a pale stripe extending from the eye to the corner of the mouth. Western rattlesnakes are active most of the day, except in very hot weather, when they retreat into burrows made by mammals. They feed on small mammals, reptiles, and amphibians, striking and biting the prey, letting the venom kill the victim, and then ingesting it. Much caution is advised around these snakes: Although they usually avoid humans, if surprised they can inflict a painful or lethal bite.

Snapping Turtle, *Chelydra serpentina*
Family Chelydridae (Snapping Turtles)
Size: Up to 14" (carapace)
Range: Eastern Colorado
Habitat: Most freshwater environments, especially with plentiful water plants

The snapping turtle is large and stocky, with a relatively small shell for its body size, a long, tapered tail, and a massive head with powerful jaws. The color is variable but usually some shade of brown, often obscured by a coating of algae. The feet are strong, with long claws. Snapping turtles may rest underwater on muddy bottoms, or bask on rocks in the sun to warm themselves. They forage for a wide variety of prey, including plants, insects, aquatic invertebrates, small mammals, amphibians, and birds. Use caution around this turtle, as it can give a painful bite.

Painted Turtle, *Chrysemys picta*
Family Emydidae (Pond and Box Turtles)
Size: Up to 10" (carapace)
Range: Northeastern Colorado
Habitat: Ponds, lakes, marshes, slow-moving streams

The painted turtle is a widespread and common pond turtle, found from coast to coast in the United States. The carapace is oval, flattened, keeless, smooth, and has a continuous (not serrated) rear margin. The rear legs are flattened, with webbed toes, and the front legs are stumpy, with long claws (longer in males). The color of the carapace is olive brown to blackish, with yellowish to reddish variegations and scute margins. The skin on the legs and head is dark green with yellow stripes, and the plastron is yellow to orange, with a broad black pattern in the center. Male painted turtles are considerably smaller than females. Highly aquatic and active during the day, these turtles are often found basking on logs or rocks in groups, and feed on all manner of aquatic prey, including plants, invertebrates, and small amphibians.

AMPHIBIANS

Northern Cricket Frog, *Acris crepitans*
Family Hylidae (Tree Frogs)
Size: Up to 1.5"
Range: Northeastern Colorado
Habitat: Warm, shallow streams and ponds

The northern cricket frog is a small, ground-dwelling member of the tree frog family. It has bumpy, rough skin and partially webbed rear feet. Its color varies considerably, being some combination of mottled and patchy browns, greens, blacks, and reds, with a paler belly. There is often a distinct triangular mark between its eyes and a whitish stripe below the eyes that extends to the front legs. Though not a climber, the cricket frog is an excellent jumper (it can leap up to 3 feet) and swimmer. Active during the day in water and on the ground, it sometimes basks along shores in groups. The cricket frog feeds on small insects and aquatic invertebrates. Its voice is a steely, clicking sound, presumably resembling that of a cricket.

Western Chorus Frog, *Pseudacris triseriata*
Family Hylidae (Tree Frogs)
Size: Up to 1.5"
Range: Throughout Colorado
Habitat: Grassy areas near water, meadows, marshes, lakes

The chorus frog is a small member of the tree frog family, although it is largely a ground-dweller. Its body is plump, with a relatively large head, thin legs, and unwebbed toes. Its skin is smooth, olive to brown and pale below, and typically there are three broad, darker stripes along the back, which may be broken or nearly absent in some populations. A dark stripe runs through the eye, and a whitish line above the jaw. Active in the evening and through the night, the common name is derived from the short, trilled calls that the frog often sings in the company of others (as in a chorus). These frogs lurk in vegetation, around water, and under logs and rocks, seeking out small prey such as insects, worms, and spiders.

American Bullfrog, *Lithobates catesbeiana*
Family Ranidae (True Frogs)
Size: Up to 6"
Range: Eastern Colorado
Habitat: Ponds and lakes with dense vegetation

North America's largest frog, the bullfrog is squat and heavy bodied, with massive rear legs that allow quick, strong leaps and strong swimming. Its smooth skin is green to brownish green, with brown or gray mottling or spotting and a pale belly. Its large external eardrums are located just behind the eyes. Bullfrogs are mostly nocturnal, and are always found in or near a body of water. Their large mouths enable them to feed on a wide variety of prey, including insects, aquatic invertebrates, and even small mammals and birds.

Wood Frog, *Lithobates sylvatica*
Family Ranidae (True frogs)
Size: Up to 3"
Range: North-central Colorado
Habitat: Woodlands, grassy areas

The wood frog is widespread in the northerly latitudes, ranging as far north as the Arctic Circle—the only North American frog to do so. The skin is brown to greenish overall, with darker spots and mottling, and sometimes with a pale stripe down the back. The dorsolateral folds are distinct, and the belly is pale. Most striking is a black mask that extends across the eyes to the eardrums, and a pale stripe on the upper jaw. Adapted to a mainly terrestrial existence, the wood frog's rear toes are not fully webbed. Quite active and excellent jumpers, they feed on a wide variety of insects, other invertebrates, and plant matter. To survive in cold climates, wood frogs have exquisite physiology that allows most of their body tissue to freeze during the winter hibernation, then thaw as spring arrives.

Great Plains Toad, *Anaxyrus cognatus*
Family Bufonidae (Toads)
Size: Up to 4.5"
Range: Northern and eastern Colorado
Habitat: Prairies, desert scrub, farmlands, areas with loose soils and ephemeral water sources

The Great Plains toad is large and plump. It is a burrowing toad, and may spend much of its life underground, especially during dry weather. The two raised cranial crests atop the head converge in front to form a knob on the upper snout, while in back they diverge to the parotid glands. The skin is rough, covered with small warts, and colored pale brown, gray, or olive. Symmetrically arranged darker blotches with light borders appear across the back. The belly is unmarked white. Active at night, Great Plains toads eat earthworms and insects, especially the destructive cutworm that can devastate crops. In breeding season, during summer rains, males vocalize a long, drawn-out, high-pitched trilling song.

Western Spadefoot, *Spea hammondi*
Family Scaphiopodidae (Spadefoot Toads)
Size: Up to 2.5"
Range: Far southern Colorado
Habitat: Dry, grassy plains, sandy or gravelly areas

The spadefoots are so called because they possess a small, hard, spadelike projection on the bottom of each hind foot, which is used to help excavate burrows. The western spadefoot has a squat body, large, protruding eyes with vertical pupils, smoother skin than the true toads, and no parotid glands. The color is gray, brown, or greenish, with variable darker blotches and spots that sometimes form indistinct lines down the back; the spots often contain orange-tipped warts. The belly is unmarked white. Spadefoots remain in burrows during the day and in times of dry weather, emerging at night and during periods of rain to feed on a variety of insects and worms. They have a quick breeding schedule, suitable for producing young in temporary, seasonal pools. The skin of these toads secretes a chemical that can cause allergy symptoms in humans.

Tiger Salamander, *Ambystoma tigrinum*
Family Ambystomatidae (Mole Salamanders)
Size: Up to 13"
Range: Throughout Colorado
Habitat: Quite varied: forests, grasslands, sage land, wetlands

The tiger salamander is the largest land-dwelling salamander in the world, with a wide variation in color and pattern. The body is robust and rounded; it has a broad, blunt head, small eyes, smooth, shiny skin, and a long tail (longer in males). There are six recognized subspecies, each with a markedly different appearance, ranging from black or brown with yellowish crossbars or whitish spots to pale brown with black barring to pea green with black blotches. Tiger salamanders spend most of their lives in deep burrows made by rodents, emerging during late-winter rains and migrating to pools or streams to breed. They feed on insects, worms, other amphibians, and small rodents.

FISH

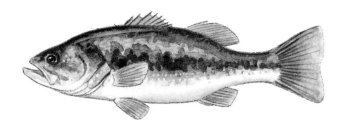

Largemouth Bass, *Micropterus salmoides*
Family Centrarchidae (Sunfish)
Size: Up to 29"
Range: Throughout Colorado
Habitat: Shallow freshwater lakes, rivers, and ponds

The largemouth bass is a favorite of anglers for its tenacious fight when hooked. It is an elongate member of the sunfish family, with a mouth that extends to the rear of the eye, two separate dorsal fins (the first spiny and the second soft), and an indented tail fin. Its color is greenish-gray above, with a blotchy, blackish lateral stripe (fading with age), and a whitish belly. Largemouth bass skulk through warmer and weedier parts of creeks or lakes, foraging for a wide variety of aquatic prey including crustaceans, insects, other fish, and frogs.

Bluegill, *Lepomis macrochirus*
Family Centrarchidae (Sunfish)
Size: Up to 10"
Range: Throughout Colorado
Habitat: Shallow lakes and rivers with aquatic plants

Also known as the "bream," the bluegill is a popular freshwater sport fish. It has an oval, highly compressed body with a small mouth, a dorsal fin that is elongated to the rear, and a slightly forked tail fin. Its color is grayish-green above, with indistinct, darker, broad vertical bars along the sides, and a dark blue-black patch on the operculum. The underparts are silvery to yellow, becoming red-orange on the chest of the spawning male. Bluegills feed on insects, insect larvae, crustaceans, and small fish. The male is illustrated.

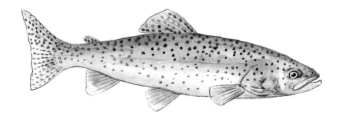

Rainbow Trout, *Oncorhynchus mykiss*
Family Salmonidae (Salmon and Trout)
Size: Up to 30" (usually smaller)
Range: Throughout Colorado
Habitat: Cool freshwater streams

This species, a member of the salmon family, has forms that exist only in freshwater streams (rainbow trout) and forms that migrate to the sea (steelhead; not found in Colorado). They are elongate, thick-bodied fish with small heads, soft fins, smooth scales, and a squared-off tail fin. Rainbow trout are greenish above, whitish below, with a pale pink section across the sides. They have extensive black spots along the back, sides, and fins. To breed, they lay eggs in the loose, gravelly bottoms of cool headwater steams. They feed on a wide variety of prey, including other fish, insects, larvae, eggs, and crustaceans. These trout are a favorite of anglers for their excellent, mild flavor.

Brown Trout, *Salmo trutta*
Family Salmonidae (Salmon and Trout)
Size: Up to 30" (usually smaller)
Range: Throughout Colorado
Habitat: Lakes and streams

Common in Colorado, the brown trout is a popular game fish that has been introduced to the state. It inhabits cool mountain regions, as well as warmer lakes and rivers at lower elevations. The long and broad body has a squared-off tail fin, a single, fleshy dorsal fin, and a small adipose fin. The coloration is a handsome combination of greenish-brown along the back, paler on the sides, and yellowish on the belly. Multitudes of dark reddish spots with white borders cover the back, sides, and dorsal fin. Brown trout spawn in headwater streams with gravel bottoms, retreating downstream or to lakes. The young feed on insects, while older fish take all manner of food items, including smaller fish.

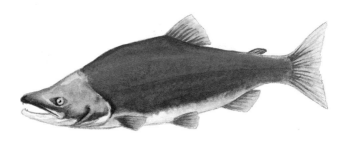

Kokanee Salmon *Oncorhynchus nerka*
Family Salmonidae (Salmon and Trout)
Size: Up to 60" (usually smaller)
Range: Mountainous Colorado
Habitat: Cool mountain lakes and reservoirs

Native to the Pacific states, where they migrate from freshwater to marine habitats and are known as sockeye salmon, the kokanee have been introduced to the lakes and streams of the Rocky Mountain region, and are prized as a game and food fish. Smaller on average than their ocean-going kin, Colorado's kokanee have a deep body with a single dorsal fin and a squared-off tail fin. Males develop a pronounced hump on their backs and hooked upper and lower mandibles. The color in mature fish is deep red along the back and sides (brightest in males) and silvery below, with a green head. Younger fish and some non-breeding individuals are plain gray overall, with darker backs. Kokanee feed principally on plankton and small insects. When breeding in the fall, they migrate upstream to spawn or may seek the gravelly shores of the lakes they inhabit year-round. The spawning male form is illustrated.

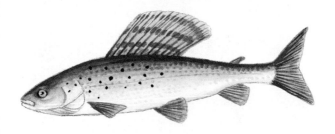

European Grayling, *Thymallus thymallus*
Family Salmonidae (Salmon and Trout)
Size: Up to 20"
Range: Mountainous Colorado
Habitat: Cool mountain lakes and reservoirs

Native to arctic regions and northern Europe, the distinctive gray-ling is a small member of the salmon family (usually less than 12" long) that can be found in cold mountain lakes and streams. It is quite unusual, with its slender body, small mouth, forked tail, and oversize, striped dorsal fin, which resembles a tall sail. The color is silvery overall, often with a blue-green or brownish tint (darkest on the back), rows of pale stripes along the sides, and sparse black spots that are most prominent on the front half of the body. Gray-ling feed on just about any food source they can swallow, includ-ing plants, insects, larvae, and crustaceans. It is a tasty game fish best attracted by small flies.

Northern Pike, *Esox lucius*
Family Esocidae (Pike and Pickerel)
Size: Up to 50" or larger
Range: Throughout Colorado
Habitat: Lakes and streams

Found throughout the higher latitudes of the Northern Hemisphere, and tolerant of almost any freshwater habitat, the northern pike is a popular sport fish because of its typically large size, aggressive fight, and mild-tasting flesh. The body is elongate and muscular, with the dorsal fin set well to the rear of the body (just above the anal fin). The pike has a pointed snout, and a large mouth laden with sharp teeth. Its color is olive-green above, white below, with irregular, oblong pale spots on its back and sides. Although the young feed primarily on insects and small crustaceans, mature fish are carnivorous, hunting by waiting and ambushing other fish, amphibians, or even birds and small mammals.

BUTTERFLIES

Pipevine Swallowtail, *Battus philenor*
Family Papilionidae (Swallowtails and Parnassians)
Size: Wingspan 3–5"
Range: Southeastern Colorado
Habitat: Woodland edges, streamsides, open fields

The pipevine swallowtail is dark, medium-size and active, with shallowly scalloped hind wings and moderate tail projections. It is poisonous to predators and thus often mimicked by other butterfly species. The upper side of the forewing is flat black and iridescent, while the upper surface of the hind wing is metallic blue (more developed in males), with pale crescent-shaped spots along its base. The underside hind wing has large, orange, submarginal spots and retains the blue sheen of the upper surface. The body is black, with small yellow spots along the sides, and the antennae are thin with clubbed tips. The caterpillar is dark, reddish brown, smooth, and lined with fleshy appendages and orange spots. The caterpillar eats the leaves of pipevines and related plants. The adult feeds on flower nectar and nutrients from mud puddles.

Western Tiger Swallowtail, *Papilio rutulus*
Family Papilionidae (Swallowtails and Parnassians)
Size: Wingspan 3–4"
Range: Throughout Colorado
Habitat: Gardens, parks, riversides, forest clearings

Among the largest of North American butterflies, the western
tiger swallowtail is common throughout its range. It is diurnal
and—typical of this family—has distinct projections or "tails" on
its hind wings. When alighted and/or feeding, the wings may
tremble. Both sexes are bright yellow above and show ragged
black stripes, like those of a tiger, along the anterior forewings,
and black marginal patterning on both fore- and hind wings. The
first submarginal spot on the hind wing is orange. The underside is
patterned similarly but is much paler yellow. Females show bright
blue posterior markings. Like the wings, the body also has black
and yellow stripes. The caterpillar is brown to greenish, smooth,
and plump. The caterpillar eats the leaves of trees, including those
from the rose, magnolia, poplar, and willow families. Adults feed
on flower nectar and the salts and moisture from puddles.

Orange Sulfur, *Colias eurytheme*
Family Pieridae (Sulfurs and Whites)
Size: Wingspan 1.5–2.5"
Range: Throughout Colorado
Habitat: Meadows, fields, farmlands, roadsides

Also known as the alfalfa butterfly, this common butterfly is often found in dense, low-flying groups over alfalfa fields, where it is often considered a pest. The upper side wings are yellow and extensively washed with bright orange. A wide, dark band occurs along the outer margins of both the fore- and hind wings, a reddish discal spot appears on the hind wing, and a distinct black discal spot sits on the forewing. The dark margin in females is broken by irregular orange markings. The underside is yellow, with a red-bordered white discal spot on the hind wing, accompanied by a smaller spot just above. The body is pale yellow below, darker above, and the club-tipped antennae are reddish. The caterpillar is thin, smooth, and green, with a pale longitudinal stripe down each side. This species is similar to the clouded or common sulfur, which has a lemon-yellow rather than an orange cast, and lacks the hind wing spot. The caterpillar eats alfalfa and clover. Adults feed on flower nectar. The adult male is illustrated.

Cabbage Butterfly, *Pieris rapae*
Family Pieridae (Sulfurs and Whites)
Size: Wingspan 1.3–1.75"
Range: Throughout Colorado
Habitat: Open fields, farmlands, roadsides

Also known as the cabbage white or small white, the cabbage butterfly is a hardy, nonnative species introduced to North America in the late 1800s and now found across the continent. The upper side wings are a plain creamy white, with gray to black apical patches, and show a distinct dark spot on the center of the forewings and upper margins of the hind wings. Females have an additional spot on the forewing, below the first. The underside is pale yellow to yellow green. Early broods of this species tend to be paler, with fewer dark markings, than late broods. The body is dark above, paler below, with long hairs, especially on the thorax. The antennae are thin and club-tipped. The caterpillar is pale green, with thin, longitudinal yellow stripes and a delicate, bumpy-hairy surface. The caterpillar eats cabbage and other plants of the mustard (Brassicaceae) family, including *Nasturtium*. Also known as a "cabbage worm," it is considered a major pest to crops. Adults feed on flower nectar. The adult female is illustrated.

Pine White, *Neophasia menapia*
Family Pieridae (Sulfurs and Whites)
Size: Wingspan 1.5–2.25"
Range: Mountainous regions
Habitat: Central and western Colorado

The pine white is small and white, with rounded wings, and is often found flying high in the canopy of pine and fir trees. The upper side wings are creamy white overall, with a dark gray costal margin, discal spot, and an outer margin broken by white spots. The hind wings have faint, darker lines along the wing veins; these are more pronounced on the undersides. The female's wings are paler than the male's, and their undersides are yellow-tinged, with thin, pinkish margins on the hind wings. The body is mottled white and gray, and the antennae are thin and club-tipped. The caterpillar is small and green, with white stripes along the top and sides. This butterfly drops from a tree on a silken thread to pupate on the ground. The caterpillar eats the needles of conifers, especially those of Douglas fir, balsam fir, Jeffrey pine, and ponderosa pine. Adults feed on flower nectar. The adult male is illustrated.

Gray Hairstreak, *Strymon melinus*
Family Lycaenidae (Blues, Coppers, Hairstreaks, and Gossamer-Wings)
Size: Wingspan 1–1.25"
Range: Throughout Colorado
Habitat: Fields, open rural areas, disturbed sites

The swift-flying gray hairstreak is the most common hairstreak in North America. Hairstreaks are so called because of the thin streaks that are usually present along the undersides of their wings. They also usually have one or two thin tails on each hind wing. The upper side wings are slate-gray overall (browner in females), with white margins. When there are two tails, they are uneven in length, and accompanied near their bases by a large orange spot above a smaller black dot. The underside is pale brown gray with black streaking, bordered with white and orange. The body is stout, grayish above and paler gray below, and the hairstreak has black-and-white dotted antennae tipped with orange. The caterpillar is pale green to brownish, plump, and covered with fine whitish hairs. The caterpillar eats the fruits, flowers, leaves, and seedpods of a variety of plants including legumes, mallow, and cotton, often boring into its food. Adults feed on flower nectar. The adult male is illustrated.

American Copper, *Lycaena phlaeas*
Family Lycaenidae (Blues, Coppers, Hairstreaks, and Gossamer-Wings)
Size: Wingspan 1–1.25"
Range: Throughout Colorado
Habitat: Meadows, roadsides, fields

The American copper is a small, beautiful, common butterfly with a fairly aggressive disposition. The wing patterning is variable, but generally the upper side is coppery-orange on the forewing, with a dark marginal band and several black spots. The hind wing is mostly blackish or dark brown, with an orange basal band, and a thin, pale margin runs all around on both wings. The undersides are similar but much paler overall. Sexes are similar, although some females may show bluish markings above the orange band on the hind wing. The body is dark brown above, pale grayish below; the butterfly has dark, club-tipped antennae dotted with white. The caterpillar is sluglike, variously colored from pale greenish to reddish, and is covered with fine hairs. The caterpillar feeds on various sorrels and docks. Adults feed on flower nectar. The adult female is illustrated.

Blue Copper, *Lycaena heteronea*
Family Lycaenidae (Blues, Coppers, Hairstreaks, and Gossamer-Wings)
Size: Wingspan 1.1–1.4"
Range: Throughout Colorado
Habitat: Alpine meadows, open brush, sage land

The blue copper is an unusual copper because of its blue color, and is sometimes confused with one of the "blue" butterflies, although the coppers are noticeably larger. The upper side wings of the male are brilliant, sky blue, with white margins, a thin, black submarginal band, and darkened veins. The female is blue-gray to brown above, with several small, dark, interior spots on both wings. The undersides of both sexes are pale grayish to yellowish with dark spotting (usually more pronounced on females). The body is stout, hairy, dark gray above and paler below. The butterfly has thin, black-and-white dotted, club-tipped antennae. The caterpillar is pale green and covered with fine, whitish hairs. The caterpillar feeds on the leaves of buckwheat. Adults feed on flower nectar, principally that of buckwheat. The adult male is illustrated.

Colorado Hairstreak, *Hypaurotis crysalus*
Family Lycaenidae (Blues, Coppers, Hairstreaks, and Gossamer-Wings)
Size: Wingspan 1.25–1.5"
Range: Throughout Colorado
Habitat: Oak woodlands, canyons, scrub

The Colorado hairstreak is one of the larger hairstreaks, and often rests high in the canopies of oak trees. Like most hairstreaks, it has wispy tails and an adjacent, shorter tail projection on the hind wings. The upper side of the wings is bright violet, with a broad, dark, blackish-brown band at the margins and thin, white edges. There are orange spots at the outer angle of the forewing, and at the base of the hind wing. The sexes are similar. Undersides are pale brown to gray, with several white "hairstreak" lines, and a jagged line on the hind wing that resembles the letter M. The body is dark gray above, lighter below; the butterfly has black-and-white dotted, thin, club-tipped antennae. The caterpillar is plump and light green, with fine, whitish hairs. The caterpillar eats mostly the leaves of Gambel oak. Adults feed on the honeydew of aphids, tree sap, and sometimes flower nectar.

Mormon Metalmark, *Apodemia mormo*
Family Riodinidae (Metalmarks)
Size: Wingspan 0.8–1.3"
Range: Western and central Colorado
Habitat: Deserts and other arid, rocky areas

The striking Mormon metalmark, a member of the group known as "checkered metalmarks," is very active, and will often rest with its wings outstretched. The female is larger than the male, with broader wings, but otherwise is similar. The upper side of the wing is rusty orange on the inner portion of the forewing and dark brown to blackish elsewhere, with extensive white spotting overall and checkered wing margins. The underside is patterned as above but set against a much paler background color. The body is dark brown above, whitish below; the butterfly has thin, club-tipped antennae and unusual green eyes. The caterpillar is plump, patterned in brown, purplish, and black, with long, thin hairs. The caterpillar eats the leaves and stems of plants in the buckwheat family (Polygonaceae). Adults feed on flower nectar, particularly that of rabbitbrush and others in the sunflower family (Asteraceae).

Common Checkered-skipper, *Pyrgus communis*
Family Hesperiidae (Skippers)
Size: Wingspan 1–1.4"
Range: Throughout Colorado
Habitat: Open areas, woodland edges, meadows, roadsides

The common checkered-skipper is widespread. It has quick, darting flight and an aggressive attitude. As with other skippers, it has a robust body, large eyes, and relatively short wings. The upper side of wings is light, slate-gray overall (in males), blackish or sometimes brownish (in females), and is extensively checkered with white spots. The wing margins are also checkered with white. The underside is paler, with similar checkering. The body is brown to gray above, mottled pale gray-and-white below; it has somewhat curving antennae tips. The caterpillar is green to brownish, with thin, dark, longitudinal stripes, and is covered with fine, short hairs. It has a dark brown head and a constricted neck area. The caterpillar eats a variety of mallows and hollyhocks. Adults feed on flower nectar.

Monarch, *Danaus plexippus*
Family Nymphalidae (Brushfoot Butterflies; Milkweed Butterflies Group)
Size: Wingspan 3–4.5"
Range: Throughout Colorado
Habitat: Sunny, open fields, as well as meadows and gardens. During migration, monarchs can be found in almost any environment.

The monarch is a large, sturdy, long-lived butterfly best known for making one of the most incredible migratory journeys in the animal kingdom—a yearly flight to Mexico in which millions of this species gather in discrete, isolated locations. The upper side of the wing is deep orange, with wide, black stripes along the veins and black margins infused with a double row of white spots. Males have narrower black vein markings than females, as well as a small, dark "sex spot" near the base of each hind wing. The underside is marked as above, but the orange is paler. The body is black with white spots on the head and thorax; the monarch has thin, club-tipped antennae. The caterpillar is fat, smooth, ringed with black, white, and yellow bands, and has black tentacles behind its head. The caterpillar eats leaves and flowers of milkweed. Adults feed on flower nectar. Both store toxins from milkweed that make them distasteful to predators. The adult male is illustrated.

Painted Lady, *Vanessa cardui*
Family Nymphalidae (Brushfoot Butterflies; Ladies Group)
Range: Throughout Colorado
Habitat: Open habitats, gardens, fields, alpine meadows

The painted lady is medium-size, wide-ranging, and common. It can be found around the world, so it is sometimes called the cosmopolitan. It has strong but erratic flight and is capable of long migrations. The upper side wings are pale orange brown with extensive black markings. A black apical region on the forewing contains several white spots, and small blue spots may be visible at the inner base of the hind wing. The underside forewing is patterned as above, but the hind wing is mottled in earth tones, with a row of submarginal eyespots. The body is speckled light and dark brown above, and is whitish below; the butterfly has thin, club-tipped antennae ending in pale dots. The caterpillar is blackish with pale yellow stripes, and is covered in fine hairs and bristles. The caterpillar eats a wide variety of plants including thistles, nettles, burdock, hollyhock, and mallow, enabling it to thrive in most areas. Adults feed on flower nectar.

Common Buckeye, *Junonia coenia*
Family Nymphalidae (Brushfoot Butterflies; True Brushfoot Group)
Size: Wingspan 1.75–2.5"
Range: Eastern Colorado
Habitat: Open fields, meadows

The common buckeye is medium-size and common. It has pronounced eyespots, which are thought to confuse and deter predators. The common buckeye tends to remain on or near the ground or near the low parts of vegetation. The upper side wings are variable shades of brown, with each wing showing one large and one small multicolored spot. There is also a creamy bar near the apex of the forewing, two orange marks in the discal cell, and scalloped patterning along the entire wing edge. The underside is paler, sometimes achieving a rose cast, with the eyespots still visible. The body is tan to dark brown; the buckeye has pale, club-tipped antennae. The caterpillar is mottled black, white, and brown, with dark stripes above, and is covered in black, branched spines. The caterpillar eats the leaves, buds, and fruit of plantains, gerardias, and snapdragons. Adults feed on flower nectar, and moisture from mud and sand.

Mourning Cloak, *Nymphalis antiopa*
Family Nymphalidae (Brushfoot Butterflies; True Brushfoot Group)
Size: Wingspan 2.25–3.5"
Range: Throughout Colorado
Habitat: Deciduous woodlands, parks, rural gardens

The mourning cloak is common, with the angular, jagged wing margins typical of the tortoiseshells. The adult overwinters in tree cavities, emerging the following spring to breed. The upper side wings are deep burgundy brown with wide, pale yellow margins. Inside the margin are light blue spots surrounded by black. The underside is dark gray with the same yellowish margin, though on this side the margin is speckled with black. The body is stout and dark brown to blackish both above and below; the butterfly has thin, club-tipped antennae. The caterpillar is black, covered with spines, and has small white dots and a row of reddish spots along the back. The caterpillar eats the leaves of a variety of broadleaf trees, including willow, poplar, elm, birch, and hackberry. Adults feed on rotting fruit, tree sap, flower nectar (rarely), and the moisture and salts in soil.

MOTHS

Polyphemus Moth, *Antheraea polyphemus*
Family Saturniidae (Giant Silk Moths)
Size: Wingspan 3.5–5.75"
Range: Throughout Colorado
Habitat: Deciduous woodlands, gardens

The Polyphemus moth is common and very large, with a heavily furred body. It is named for the mythical Cyclops, Polyphemus, who had a single eye. The upper side wings are light to dark brown overall. The forewing has a small, black-bordered, white discal eyespot, small, black apical patches, a dark submarginal line, and a reddish basal stripe. The hind wing has very large black eyespots encircling yellow, and a broad, dark, submarginal stripe. The underside is paler overall, with only a suggestion of eyespots. The body is brownish overall, above and below, with feathered antennae, which are more pronounced in the male. The caterpillar is bright green with a brown head, banded with thin yellow stripes, and dotted with orange tubercles bearing thin, dark spines. The caterpillar eats leaves from a variety of broadleaf trees, including oak, willow, apple, hawthorn, and birch. Adults do not feed. The adult male is illustrated.

Sheep Moth, *Hemileuca eglanterina*
Family Saturniidae (Giant Silk Moths)
Size: Wingspan 2–3"
Range: Throughout Colorado
Habitat: A variety of habitats, including coastal areas, mountains, woodlands, pastures, and scrubland

The sheep moth, also known as the elegant sheep moth, is found in the West and can be seen flying during the day. The wing pattern and coloration are extremely variable. Generally, the moth is rosy to pink on the forewing and yellow-orange on the hind wing, with both wings showing large, central black spots, marginal streaks, and transverse bands. In some regions, however, the dark markings are more extensive, reduced, or entirely absent. The underside wing is patterned as above. The body is long for a silk moth, with a thin abdomen. The body of the sheep moth is yellow to pinkish with a black-banded abdomen; it has feathered antennae (broader in the male). The caterpillar is blackish, often with dorsal red spots and white lines along the sides and rows of highly branched orange and black spines. The caterpillar eats plants from the rose family (Rosaceae), ceanothus, willow, and aspen. Adults do not feed. The adult male is illustrated.

Pink-spotted Hawk Moth, *Agrius cingulata*
Family Sphingidae (Sphinx Moths and Hawk Moths)
Size: Wingspan 3.5–4.75"
Range: Throughout Colorado
Habitat: Open fields, gardens

The pink-spotted hawk moth has long, narrow wings, a relatively thick, long body, and powerful flight. The forewing is cryptically patterned in an intricate design of gray, brown, black, and white, which forms a perfect camouflage on tree bark when the wings are lowered. The hind wing is grayish with black bands and flushed with pink at the base. The robust body, which has a pointed tail end, is a mottled gray brown with distinct pink spots along the sides of the abdomen. The antennae are long, pale, and feathered. The caterpillar, known as the sweet-potato hornworm, can be a pest to crops. It is large, smooth, green to brown or nearly black, with pale, oblique stripes along the sides, and has a tail horn. The caterpillar eats sweet potato and jimsonweed. The adult feeds on flower nectar with an extremely long tongue (proboscis), which allows it to probe deep into tubular flowers. Adults can also feed while hovering.

White-lined Sphinx, *Hyles lineata*
Family Sphingidae (Sphinx Moths and Hawk Moths)
Size: Wingspan 2.5– 3.5"
Range: Throughout Colorado
Habitat: A variety of habitats including fields, gardens, dry scrub

The white-lined sphinx is worldwide in distribution, and some-times referred to as the striped morning sphinx because it flies during the day as well as night. It is large-bodied, with a tapered abdomen and pointed, narrow wings. The upper side of the fore-wing is tan and dark brown, with a broad pale stripe from wing base to the tip, and white veins through the stripe. The hind wing is mostly pink, with black at the base and just inside the outer margin. The wing's underside is paler overall. The body is brown-ish with white stripes on the upper thorax and head, and has black-and-white spotting along the top and sides of the abdo-men. The antennae are long, with compact feathering. The cater-pillar is plump, smooth, blackish with variable amounts of yellow or green stripes and spots, and has a prominent, yellow-orange tail horn. The caterpillar eats a variety of plants, including apple, elm, evening primrose, and tomato. The adult feeds on flower nectar, using its very long proboscis to probe deep into flowers.

Garden Tiger Moth, *Arctia caja*
Family Erebidae (Tiger Moths and Allies)
Size: Wingspan 2–2.75"
Range: East of the Continental Divide
Habitat: A variety of habitats, especially damp areas, meadows, and streamsides

The garden tiger moth is a beautiful, medium-size moth with nocturnal habits and quite variable wing coloration. In general, the upper side of the forewing consists of a contrasting mosaic of reddish or dark brown patches over a white background. The hind wing is bright orange, with large, black-rimmed blue spots and a pale margin. With the forewings folded down, the butterfly is camouflaged in grasses and brush, but when alarmed it flashes the brilliant hind wing to frighten predators. The body is dark brown above on the head and thorax, with a red collar at the neck, and orange on the abdomen, with broken, dark blue bands. It is mostly brownish-orange below, and has pale, compact antennae. The caterpillar is of the "woolly bear" type, densely covered in long, pale-tipped black bristles with shorter reddish bristles near the base and at the neck. The caterpillar eats a wide variety of herbaceous and woody plants, including blackberry, clover, plum, plantain, birch, and apple.

Isabella Tiger Moth, *Pyrrhartia isabella*
Family Erebidae (Tiger Moths and Allies)
Size: Wingspan 1.75–2.5"
Range: Throughout Colorado
Habitat: Open, deciduous woodlands, grasslands, gardens, parks

The Isabella tiger moth is common and medium-size, and is most often recognized in its larval form, the "woolly bear" caterpillar. The adult has relatively long, pointed forewings, which are colored light yellow-brown overall and sparsely marked with faint bars near the outer and medial sections. Variable numbers of small, dark spots are found on the interior and outer margin. The hind wing of the female is tinged orange to pink, whereas that of the male is pale yellow. The body is orange brown, with a hairy, tufted, upper thorax, dark spots along the upper abdomen, thin, pale antennae, and black legs. The caterpillar is plump and covered with fuzzy, fine hairs. It is black with a wide, orange-brown central section. The caterpillar eats a wide variety of herbaceous and woody plants, including maples, clover, sunflowers, elm, and grasses.

Carpenterworm Moth, *Prionoxystus robiniae*
Family Cossidae (Carpenter Moths)
Size: Wingspan 1.75–3.25"
Range: Throughout Colorado
Habitat: Deciduous woodlands, rural areas with host tree species

The carpenterworm moth is large and nocturnal, with a relatively large body, long, narrow, triangular forewings, and reduced hind wings, similar to the sphinx moths. The forewings are translucent, intricately mottled and spotted in dark gray and white. The hind wing of the male is blackish near the base and margin and yellow orange at the outer half. In females, the hind wing is mostly black. The body is mottled dark gray and white, matching the wing color, with a darker abdomen that is quite pointed at the tail end in males, and fatter in females. The antennae are feathered: thick in males, thin in females. The caterpillar, sometimes called the locust borer, may take three to four years to pupate. It is smooth, ranges from pale green to reddish, and has dark spots along the sides. The caterpillar eats a variety of broadleaf trees, including oak, willow, locust, ash, and maple. It bores tunnels into the wood of these trees and feeds therein, and can cause much damage to lumber trees.

Index

Index

About the Author/Illustrator

Todd Telander is a naturalist/illustrator/ artist living in Walla Walla, Washington. He has studied and illustrated wildlife since 1989, while living in California, Colorado, New Mexico, and Washington. He graduated from the University of California, Santa Cruz, with degrees in biology, environmental studies, and scientific illustration, and has since illustrated numerous books and other publications, including books in FalconGuides' Scats and Tracks series. His wife, Kirsten Telander, is a writer, and they have two sons, Miles and Oliver. His work can be viewed online at toddtelander.com and at telandergallery.com.